Nanny Notes on Toddlers

Books 1 - 4

Nanny P

Copyright © 2013 Nanny P
All rights reserved.
ISBN: 0615882153
ISBN-13: 978-0615882154

Table of Contents

A Note From Nanny P 7

Nanny P's Blueprint for Toilet Training 11

You Make The Difference So Prepare Yourself First 13

How To Prepare Your Child For Potty Training 15

Girls & Boys - What Are The Differences? 19

How To Know When Your Child Is Ready 21

Method 1: Basic Potty Training 25

Method 2: Potty Training In 2 Days - Really? 27

Method 3: Potty Training Dolls 29

How To Deal With Resistance 31

Potty Training Equipment List 33

Resources 35

Nanny P's Blueprint for Getting Your Toddler to Eat 39

Starting Off With The Right Mindset 41

Nutrition: Healthy Foods For Your Toddler 43

What's In The Cupboards? 47

How To Handle Sweets 51

Reward Your Child For Trying New Foods 55

Toddler Eating Strategies 57

Strategy 1: Getting Sneaky With Veggies 59

Strategy 2: Getting The Kids Involved With Grocery Shopping 61

Strategy 3: Getting The Kids Involved With Cooking 63

Strategy 4: Create Theme Nights 65

Strategy 5: Planning Menus Together 67

Strategy 6: Choosing Foods of Certain Colors 69

Strategy 7: Starting A Garden 73

A Word About Good Table Manners 75

>   Get Started!..79
>
>   Resources 81

Nanny P's Blueprint for Getting Your Toddler to Sleep 85

>   Starting Off With The Right Mindset: Prepare Yourself First.....................87
>
>   How Much Sleep Does Your Child Need?..89
>
>   Putting All The Pieces Together...91
>
>   Tip 1: Nutrition and Exercise 93
>
>   Tip 2: Napping 95
>
>   Tip 3: Avoiding Stimulation Before Bed 97
>
>   Tip 4: Consistent Bedtime..99
>
>   Tip 5: Routine Before Bed..101
>
>   Tip 6: A Nice Sleeping Environment..103
>
>   Dealing With Toddler Sleep Issues 105
>
>   Issue 1: Not Wanting to go to Bed 107
>
>   Issue 2: Wanting to Sleep with Parents..111
>
>   Issue 3: Not Sleeping Through The Night 113
>
>   Issue 4: Bed Wetting...115
>
>   Issue 5: Room Sharing with a Sibling..117
>
>   A Quick Note About Bedtime Routines When Sharing Rooms 118
>
>   Issue 6: Early Risers 119
>
>   Young Toddlers Still Breastfeeding..121
>
>   From Crib to Toddler Bed 123
>
>   Potential Medical Issues...125
>
>   Dealing with Changes in Routine 127
>
>   A Word About Co-Sleeping Option 129
>
>   Sweet Dreams! 131
>
>   Resources 133

Nanny P's Blueprint for Raising Confident Children 141

Self-Esteem vs Self-Confidence 143

Self-Esteem From A - Z 145

Your Role As A Parent 151

Strategies For Boosting Self-Esteem In Your Child 155

Strategy 1: Encouragement & Praise 157

Strategy 2: Show Genuine Interests In Your Child's Activities 159

Strategy 3: Focus On The Positive 161

Strategy 4: Listen To What Your Child Has To Say 163

Strategy 5: Encourage Dreams 165

Strategy 6: Encourage Independence 167

Strategy 7: Don't Forget To Say "I Love You" 169

Strategy 8: Stop Telling Your Child What They Should Not Do 171

Strategy 9: Consistent Boundaries & Discipline 173

Strategy 10: Let Your Child Know That Everyone Fails Sometimes 175

Strategy 11: Monitor What Your Child Is Exposed To 179

Strategy 12: Show Off Your Child's Artistic Flair! 181

Strategy 13: Play Dates & Socialization Skills 183

Start Today And Create A Brighter Future For Your Child! 187

Next Steps 189

Books For Kids 191

A Note From Nanny P

Dear Parent,

I want to welcome you to "Nanny Notes on Toddlers" and, first of all, mention that I believe that you have THE most important job that one can have….

…that would be the job of raising children that are happy, healthy and self-confident.

In my 12+ years of full-time nanny experience, I've had the privilege of working with multiple families and various ages of children.

I know that raising children can be challenging, exhausting and incredibly rewarding. The job of parenting toddlers can come with its own set of challenges and you may find yourself dealing with what many call the "terrible twos".

In this series, called Nanny Notes on Toddlers, I tackle some of the most common issues that parents deal with when it comes to raising children of the ages 1-3 years old. These topics include toilet training, eating, sleeping and raising toddlers that are confident.

Nanny P blueprints are written with the busy parent in mind. I've designed each blueprint to tackle a specific issue in a short and concise way so that you do not need to spend time reading through a lot of other material to find tips and methods for the specific topic you are looking to address.

Many of the tips and methods found here are the results of my own experience, that of my fellow nannies and also what I've learned from the amazing parents that I've had the opportunity to work for.

My own philosophy of childcare is that children need adults in their lives who'll give them:
- love
- discipline
- guidance
- a safe environment (physically and emotionally)
- fun and creativity
- motivation, vision and self confidence

I design each of my blueprints with these principles in mind.

Each book is designed be read on its own. They are meant to be blueprints for helping you parent your toddler in ways that will have your child feeling happy and confident as he or she tackles these important milestones and issues.

I very much appreciate your reviews and comments so thank you in advance for taking a moment to leave one for this book.

I wish you much success in parenting and having fun with your amazing toddler!

Sincerely,
Nanny P

Sign up for our mailing list to be alerted of new titles and special offers and get a FREE report called "Fun Activities For Young Kids!"

NannyP.com

Nanny Notes on Toddlers

Nanny P's
Blueprint For
Toilet Training

Nanny P's Blueprint for Toilet Training

Nanny P

You Make The Difference So Prepare Yourself First

If the television show "Family Feud" surveyed 100 parents of toddlers and asked, "What are the top five most frustrating things they've had to experience raising young children?" I'd be willing to bet, potty training is going to be high on the list with "beans up the nose" not too far behind!

The one thing that can make your child's potty training experience a positive and successful one is you. That's because your child will pick up on your energy and take cues directly from you. Learning how to go to the potty on their own is a big step for your child. For some children it's almost as scary as the "monster living in their closet" and it may affect their self confidence.

Are You Ready?

Before you begin the potty training process it would be a good idea to prepare yourself first. I've helped many parents over the years potty train their kids. Once they learned to allow their child to work through the process it made all the difference in the world. The joy of seeing that light bulb moment when the parent and child both "get it" is priceless. See, you're not just potty training, you're teaching your child how to be independent.

The excitement and look in those little eyes after they finally learn how to go to the potty on their own, is almost as exciting as the Publisher Clearing House prize patrol rolling up to your front door! Okay maybe not. But pretty close!

Maintaining control of your emotions and being careful not to lose your temper if your child isn't learning fast enough, prevents you from hurting your child's feelings and hampering their success.

Easy Does It

Patience on your part is going to be really important because every child is different. Some will understand the process and figure it out quickly but other children may take a lot longer. In either case, you'll need to allow your child to move at their own pace. Don't worry, with the methods I'll share, you'll know if you're moving too fast for your child. You will be able to make adjustments along the way.

Just remember to always stay calm, even when your child has an accident. I'll also give you tips on how to handle accidents without traumatizing your child.

Mistakes Happen

Okay. Just so you don't freak out, I'm going to let you in on a little secret.

Ready?

You're going to make mistakes! Just like your child probably won't get it right the first time, the second time or even the tenth time. You're going to make mistakes too. There really isn't one right way to potty train a child. You may try one method and find it's not working. That's okay. You can always try something else or even combine methods.

Now that we've gotten you squared away, let's take a look at a few important steps to get your child ready for potty training.

How To Prepare Your Child For Potty Training

In the last chapter, I gave you some tips to prepare yourself for the potty training process. Before you jump right in you'll also need to prepare your little one for what's ahead.

Show & Tell

Take time to sit down with your child and explain what it means to go to the potty. You can tell him or her that they are getting to be a big boy or girl just like mommy and daddy, or an older sibling if applicable. Tell him or her that everyone goes to the potty and now they will learn how to go too.

The important thing to remember is to make it very relaxed for your child. Allow him or her to explore the bathroom as well as the toilet itself with you present of course. You could let them flush the toilet while explaining how everything gets washed away. Let your child see how the lid lifts up and down.

You may also want to explain what the toilet paper is for and how to wash their hands after using the potty. You will have to work on each step with them several times before they're able to do them on their own.

Keep it simple so you don't overwhelm.

Let him or her know they won't be wearing diapers anymore. That's because "big kids" get to wear underwear instead. Then show them a pair. Use the excitement in your voice to help your child understand how great "being a big boy or girl" will be. It will be reassuring and help with their confidence.

Clothing

Clothes that are easy to remove will be very important as you and your child move through the training. Small children have small bladders. So when they've got to go they may not be able to hold it long enough if they have to deal with too many buttons, belts or snaps.

So, during potty training plan to dress your child in clothing that doesn't require him or her to struggle to get them off. This will be less stressful for the both of you.

Training Underwear

Choosing whether to go with regular underwear, training pants or Pull-ups is really up to you. But whichever you choose, do so consistently. If you start out with Pull-ups then stick with them throughout the training. Children get used to a certain way of doing something rather quickly. Changing the underwear type in the middle of potty training can be confusing to him or her. Always keep plenty of training underwear handy. Putting a diaper on your child just until you can make it to the store even for a short period of time, could also cause confusion. So try to avoid this as much as possible.

Diaper Wearing Exception

The exception to this rule where diapers are concerned is during the night when your child is sleeping. Wearing a diaper at night can help a lot because of night time bed wetting. Even when your child masters going to the bathroom during the day, it will be several months before they will be developed enough physically to go to the bathroom during the night.

Let Your Child Help Set Up Equipment & Choose Training Pants

Children love being your little helper! So let them help set up their training potty. You could let them place it in a specific area of the bathroom and other common rooms. Show them how to use a step stool for example. Help them practice stepping up and down. You might also teach them how to step up to the sink so they can wash their hands. Teaching them how to do it will be a big step for them. It will help them feel a lot more at ease about the entire process.

You could also let your child choose between different kinds of colors or designs when it comes to training underwear. Let them feel like they have a say in choosing the kind they like the best.

This is a great way for them to associate something positive with the experience.

I've put together a list of equipment you will need in order to get the most benefit out the process. You'll find a list in the Potty Training Equipment List section.

A Word About Maintaining A Routine For Your Child

It's going to be really important to be consistent and establish a routine during the potty training process. This is a scary time for your child. He or she will have a better chance at being successful with their training if they know what to expect from you.

So you've got to make an effort to do things the same way over and over again. It will help them build confidence and reduce their stress.

Next, let's take a look at the differences between boys and girls when it comes to potty training.

Nanny P

Girls & Boys - What Are The Differences?

Do Girls Really Learn Faster Than Boys?

In my opinion and based on my own experiences, boys aren't slower than girls when it comes to potty training. They simply learn differently than girls. The anatomical differences between boys and girls has a lot to do with the speed at which each learns.

If a male child is being raised in a single parent home by his mother, for example, it's likely he'll take a little longer to learn how to "use his equipment" if there isn't another male present in the home. Let's face it, moms simply can't demonstrate how a boy goes potty better than a male can.

Young children learn a lot by watching and then imitating what they see. That doesn't mean moms can't train their sons to go to the potty. It just may take their sons a little longer to catch on.

If you are a single mom raising a son, you can ask other male family members to help you.

Get Dad Involved!

On the other hand, in a two parent household some dads leave the responsibility of potty training up to the moms. Dads can help by participating in the training by doing "show and tell" with their sons. For example showing them how to stand when they need to urinate and sit to have bowel movements.

Special Tip For Boys

A good game to play with boys is the "Aim & Shoot Game." When your son has to pee, toss a few pieces of dry cereal in the toilet. Then tell him to "aim for the cereal and pee!" It's a great way to help him learn how to hold his penis and control where he pees. Plus young children can get bored pretty quickly. Instead of making pee art all over your bathroom he'll be distracted with the game of aiming for the cereal in the toilet.

Special Tip For Girls

Since females don't stand to use the bathroom. Moms can easily demonstrate to girls how to use the potty properly.

How To Know When Your Child Is Ready

How do you know when it's time to start potty training? Well, I can tell you after working with dozens of parents over the years, that's a million dollar question! The best answer I can give you is this.

It depends on your child. See every child is different. Some may be ready at 2 years while others may take another year or longer. So there's no hard and fast rule that says it must be by a specific age. However, it's common for many children to start right around 2 - 2 1/2. Don't worry if your child starts later. That's perfectly fine.

You'll find a lot of information out there on how to potty train your child really fast. While those methods can work, they don't necessarily work for every child. The last thing you want to do is rush your child before they're ready. Instead let him or her learn how to go to the potty at their own pace.

Look For Signs Your Child Is Ready

There are a few ways to figure out whether or not your angel is ready for potty training. Here are the most common signs to look for.

"Hey Mom? Dad?...I Gotta Go!"

Okay so most toddlers won't be quite that clear. But if your child verbally tells you in their own way that they need to potty. Or if your child is frantically pointing or grabbing their private parts desperately trying to get your attention. That's a pretty good sign they are ready for potty training.

"Whew! Get This Wet Diaper Off Of Me...Now!"

If your toddler starts giving you the "mean mug" every time they wet their diaper or try to pull it off when wet, that's a good indication they may be ready to ditch the diaper and move up to training pants.

"Quick Change Artist"

If you've got a child that can easily pull their pants up and down with little help from you. It's possible they're ready for training. That's because during the process he or she will be learning how to adjust their clothing before they potty.

"Are You Talking To Me?"

Communication on a level your child can understand is so important. If your child can follow basic directions from you, they should be able to start the potty training process. If you feel they're too distracted or just can't figure out what you want them to do, then it's okay to delay potty training until later.

Is Your Child Physically Ready?

Monitor how long your child stays dry throughout the day. A good rule of thumb is if he or she can go 2 or more hours without wetting themselves that's long enough to start training. But that's only during the daytime. Children take a lot longer to master going to the potty at night during sleep. So while your child may be fine during the day, it may be some time before they get to the point where they are no longer wetting the bed at night. It's normal, so try and be patient.

Young toddlers also have to learn to recognize the physical cues from their body that tells him or her it's time to go to the bathroom.

That's a lot to figure out when they've spent their entire young lives being taught to go in a diaper. So again, observe your child to see if they've reached the point where they are ready to take this big step.

Finally, if your child meets the criteria I just mentioned see if he or she can get on and off the potty on their own. If so, you can feel comfortable getting them started.

When You Should Wait

Just as there are common signs that signal a child is ready for potty training there are other times when you should wait.

Change can be very stressful even for a 2 year old. Moving to a new home, getting a new babysitter, divorce or even that fun trip to see Mickey Mouse can be very stressful for a child. If there are any major changes to your child's environment coming up it would be best to wait until things get back to normal before potty training.

Time To Get Started

Now on to the actual training methods. I wanted to be as helpful as possible as you go through the training, so I've included three of the most common methods for potty training toddlers. I'll cover specific tips for each and the most common problems and how to solve them.

Nanny P

Method 1: Basic Potty Training

There are literally dozens of potty training methods to choose from, all of which have worked successfully for millions of parents and their children. The trick of course is figuring out which method is the right one for your child. That's where you come in. No one knows your child's personality traits better than you do. How your child learns to do other activities may be your best indicator on the best method to try.

Don't worry about making a mistake and choosing the wrong one. There really isn't a wrong method. If you try one and it doesn't work out just try again with another method until you find something that does work. Be patient. You and your child will figure it out together.

Let's take a look at one of the most basic and most common methods to successfully potty training your child.

Slow & Steady Method

Step One
One of the keys to successful potty training is making it a fun experience for your child. One way to do so is to buy a potty chair and tell your child it is just for him or her. This will give your child the impression that it's a really good thing to have and that it belongs to them and no one else. Place it in your bathroom.

Step Two
For the next couple of weeks let your child sit on the potty chair fully clothed when you go to the bathroom. Each time they go to the bathroom with you, they are learning the process a little bit more. They may ask you questions. Answer as simply as possible while also letting him or her know that they will get a chance to be just like mommy or daddy one day. It's common for young children to lose interest quickly. So if your child wants to leave, it's okay to let them do so. You want to associate positive experiences and fun, so never force them to stay.

Step Three
Once your child has gotten used to sitting on their potty, you can now have them sit without a diaper. Don't be concerned with whether or not they pee or poop. For now just let them get used to the idea of being without a diaper. When your child pees or has a bowel movement in their diaper casually take them to the bathroom and empty the waste into their potty chair. Then in a reassuring and lighthearted tone, tell your child that pee pee and poop goes in their potty chair.

Step Four
At this point you should take your child to their potty chair several times throughout the day. This step should only be done if you are sure your child clearly understands you when you tell them where their poop should go. If they do not you may need to spend a longer period of time on steps two and three. Or it could simply mean your child isn't ready for potty training right now.

Step Five
If you think your child is getting more and more comfortable with the process so far, you can remove the diaper and pants for short periods during the day. Then encourage your child to go to the "potty chair" to pee or poop.

Once your child is starting to get the hang of "going" you can then move up to training pants. You need to show your child how to raise and lower the training pants. It may take your child awhile to make the association of lowering their training pants to go potty or they may get it right away.

The Keys To Success

How long will it take? Again, that depends on your child. If you're not seeing your child progress, you may need to either try another method or combine methods. In either case, patience is very important. Keep the training fun and lighthearted for your child even when he or she has an accident. Keep encouraging your child and eventually they'll get it.

Method 2: Potty Training In 2 Days - Really?

A lot of parents would be more than happy to avoid weeks or months of accidents and other frustrations associated with potty training. I mean really, why spend all that time if a child can be potty trained in just 2 days right?

Well, depending on the method, the child, you and any number of other factors, those 2 days can actually be the result of several hours or weeks of prior preparation. That means you'll still have to cover the basics with your child including introducing him or her to the bathroom environment and allowing them to watch you go so they can learn from you.

The 2 day method requires you to do the following steps throughout the entire 2 days. If you're working a full time job, you'll need to take two full days off in order to get the best results with this method. Also keep in mind, preparation for both you and your child is always important. So don't skip that. Review the sections on preparing yourself for potty training as well as the section on prepping your child if you're unsure.

How To Potty Train Your Child in 2 Days

Step One
Let your child go to the bathroom with you so they can see what goes on in the bathroom. Be sure to place a potty chair in the bathroom as well. Remember they will learn from watching you. If you have a boy, get Dad involved in the training. In each case, make sure you keep the experience lighthearted and don't make a big deal out of it. Especially in the beginning your child's attention span will be short. Don't get upset if your little angel gets bored quickly. Just keep repeating the process over and over again, each time you go to the bathroom.

Place additional potties in common areas throughout your home.

Step Two
Remove your child's diaper and pants. Put a comfortable shirt on that's long enough to cover up their private parts. Then let them run around as they normally do.

Then every 10 - 15 minutes place them on the nearest potty. Don't ask if they need to pee. Just lead them to the potty and have them sit. One parent I know used a bell to signal when it was time to go to the potty. Every 10 minutes or so she would ring the bell and casually sit her child on the potty. After a few times the child would hear the bell and go sit on their own. You can also use an alarm clock or a simple kitchen timer.

Step Three
When your child does pee or poop in the potty, give praise. Don't go over the top. Just be calm, smile and tell them how they are doing it exactly the way mommy, daddy and their bigger sister and or brother go potty too. If they have older siblings young children idolize them and love to be just like them, so use this to your advantage. In fact, if you have older children they can also help in the training by also showing your toddler how to use the potty.

Step Four
Once you've done the steps outlined above for 2 days, introduce training pants to your son or daughter. Make him or her feel proud that they can now wear the same kind of underwear other big boys and girls wear.

The Keys To Success

Consistency and a lot of patience are the keys to success using this method. You may get tired of hearing that bell or alarm going off every 10 minutes and want to stop the training, but your child needs you to be consistent. Otherwise you may find he or she will resist the training putting you back at square one. If your toddler doesn't respond to this training method, spend more time in the preparation phase and then try again another time when you feel your toddler is ready.

Method 3: Potty Training Dolls

This potty training method has been around since the 70's. The method involves the use of specially designed dolls that can actually wet themselves. The dolls help your child learn what happens when the doll pees. Also children can teach the dolls how to go potty. This actually helps the child learn about the potty training process by role playing and eventually they begin to understand how to go themselves.

You can purchase potty training dolls for both boys and girls.

How To Use Potty Training Dolls

Step One
There are dozens of different potty training dolls to choose from. It would be a good idea to let your child choose the one he or she likes the best.

Step Two
Once you purchase the doll you can begin the potty training process. Follow the same preparation tips I gave you in the How To Prepare Your Child For Potty Training section of this book. Allow your child to go to the bathroom with you. Your child will learn by watching what you do. Then incorporate the doll into the process by showing your child how to give the doll water.

Step Three
Each doll comes with its own potty. After your child gives the doll water, show them how to place the doll on the potty. The doll is designed to wet itself. In time your child will begin to understand the association between eating, drinking and going to the potty.

Step Four
Another effective idea is to have your child sit on their potty next to the doll's potty chair. This will help reinforce the potty training and may make your child feel more confident.

Step Five
The more your child "teaches" the doll how to go to the potty, eventually he or she will begin to imitate the same behavior themselves.

The Keys To Success

Don't give up! If your child isn't warming up to this method don't worry. Try one of the other methods or combine a couple. Just be sure to observe your child and be really sure they're ready to continue with training. Never force it and slow it down if you have to. The potty training dolls also come with additional tips on incorporating them in your child's training.

How To Deal With Resistance

It's not unusual for a child to become resistant to potty training. Knowing why your child is resisting or regressing their potty training can help you and your child deal with it better.

Reasons Why Your Child Is Resisting

Have you recently moved to a new home?

Divorce?

Did something happen during the process that just caused your child to freak out? In this case, he or she may associate something negative with potty training and this may cause resistance. Sometimes things you and I may not think much about can be scary for a child. For instance, maybe the lighting in the bathroom is too dim causing ordinary objects to look weird and scary.

You never know.

If your child gets nervous every time he or she approaches the bathroom, try to talk to your child to find out what's bothering him or her then take steps to ease their fears.

If none of the above match your circumstances it could be your child is just not ready and may be stubborn and difficult.

It happens.

If you suspect there may be a medical reason discuss your concerns with your child's pediatrician.

Other reasons include fear of the toilet itself. Maybe the flushing noise scares your child.

Confusion Can Lead To Resistance

It's okay to have other members help with potty training just make sure everyone is on the same page. That means everyone should be using the same method. Otherwise your child will become confused and stressed and will begin to resist the training.

What To Do If Your Child Is Resisting Potty Training

First, change the method you're using. Children have their own way of expressing themselves. It could be your method of choice just doesn't sit well with him or her. Or maybe you're just moving too fast and your child is getting frustrated. Try slowing the process down and see how your child responds.

Rewards

Make your child feel proud when he or she does manage to go to the potty by rewarding them in some way. Maybe create an award system that gives him or her a special gift if they potty successfully on their own after a certain number of times.

But if your child has an accident, do not punish him or her. While you shouldn't praise your child when they have an accident, you don't want to make him or her feel like they've committed a crime either. Just be calm about it and let your child know you still love them and you know they'll do better the next time.

Take A Break

If changing the method or slowing the process down doesn't seem to work, consider stopping the training altogether. Your child just may not be ready. It may be several days, weeks or even months before your child can start the process again.

Potty Training Equipment List

Having the right equipment can make a world of difference when you're ready to begin the training process, so I've put together a list of the most important items you'll need to get the job done. I've included a brief description for each potty training aid, plus links to the actual products in the Resources section of this book.

Potty Training Chairs

In addition to having a potty chair in your main bathroom, you'll want to have one in any other bathroom you'll be using. Plus you may want to put additional chairs in the areas of your home you spend the most time with your child and other family members. Young bladders may not be able to make it all the way up the stairs, down the hall and two doors to the right! The easier you can make potty training for your child the better.

Step Stools

In every bathroom where the child has a potty chair there should be a step stool. This will make it easier for your child to get on and off the toilet as well as to wash their hands.

Toilet Seats

These are great for helping children adapt to adult toilets when training. Some come with built in handles on the sides to help toddlers maintain their balance. They are useful for both girls and boys.

Potty Training Dolls

If you choose to go this route, there are dozens of high quality potty training dolls available. You can choose either male or female dolls.

Although every manufacturer's doll may work differently from one doll to the next, the principle is basically the same. The doll is given water and or "toy food." After awhile the diaper will become wet. You can then teach your child about potty training using the doll as an example. Each doll also comes with its own potty. Your child will be able to relate better seeing the doll as being a lot like themselves with a potty.

Potty Training Book

Done!...Nanny P has you covered on this one!

Training Underwear

Specifically look for training underwear your child may like. Maybe her favorite action hero or his favorite animals. You'll need to have several on hand…at least a dozen so you don't run out.

Rewards

I mentioned in the section on How To Deal With Resistance the importance of rewarding your child when they're successful at potty training. Pick up some gold stars or fun stickers. Each time your child goes potty give him or her a sticker as a reward. You can also buy sticker reward sets and charts made specifically to reward during potty training.

Resources

Books for Children:

The Potty Book - For Girls
http://www.amazon.com/dp/0764152319/

Once Upon a Potty - Boy
http://www.amazon.com/dp/1554072832/

A Potty for Me!: A Lift-the-Flap Instruction Manual
http://www.amazon.com/dp/0689874235/

Everyone Poops (My Body Science Series)
http://www.amazon.com/dp/192913214X/

Basic Potty Training Equipment

The following are the very basic products in each category. You can find many other products that may combine two or three into one potty training tool. There are also several elaborate items such as Disney themed chairs and other accessories.

No matter what you ultimately decide to buy always do so with safety in mind. Please use your best judgment before making your final purchase.

Potty Chairs

Summer Infant All -In -One Seat & Step Stool
http://www.amazon.com/gp/product/B000G22Y7E/

Very basic and inexpensive no frills chair for potty training. Comes in pink or blue.

Step Stools

BABYBJORN Safe Step
http://www.amazon.com/dp/B0009OLSY4/

There are a long list of stools you can buy. This is one of the most basic. 79% of those purchasing this very simple and basic potty stool rated it 4 stars or higher.

Potty Training Dolls

Once Upon A Potty Plush Doll Set for Girls
http://www.amazon.com/dp/B001DZX1HK/

Once Upon A Potty Plush Doll Set for Boys
http://www.amazon.com/dp/B001J1AZBS/

You can purchase a boy or girl version. This can be used to help your child identify more with the process itself.

Potty Training Pants

If you're uncertain on which brand to pick, stick with the brands you're most familiar with. Both Gerber and Pampers have excellent potty training pants in a variety of sizes and styles.

Potty Training Reward Stickers

My Potty Training Stickers For Boys 126 Potty Training Stickers & Charts To Motivate Toilet Training - Tracey Foote
http://www.amazon.com/dp/0970822685/

My Potty Training Stickers For Girls 126 Potty Training Stickers & Chart To Motivate Toilet Training - Tracey Foote
http://www.amazon.com/dp/0970822677/

Nanny Notes on Toddlers

Nanny P's
Blueprint For
Getting Your Toddler to Eat

Nanny P's Blueprint for Getting Your Toddler to Eat

Starting Off With The Right Mindset

As an adult you've had years to develop your taste buds and make decisions on the kinds of foods you like or don't like. It's also really easy for an adult to assume a child won't like a particular food because it's too spicy or too bland.

The first thing you've got to do is to keep an open mind. You're going to be surprised at the types of foods your child may fall in love with.

I can remember a young couple whose 2 year old loved eating very spicy foods. They were stunned and puzzled at the same time. They couldn't understand how that could be possible. Well, kids are people too. They have things they will like and things they'll hate!

The key for you as a parent is to help your child discover the foods they enjoy and introduce good healthy choices into their diets as well.

Key Points To Keep In Mind

Keep It Positive

Approach eating with the same enthusiasm you had when he or she took their first steps. It was fun and exciting right? Your child gets a kick out of pleasing you. They'll appreciate seeing your smiling face as you help them learn about and taste new foods.

Engage Your Child's Natural Curiosity

I love watching children discover new things. Children learn by exploring. In the case of food, allow your child to learn about new foods. Let him or her hold that green bean in their little hands. Encourage them to smell it and then taste it.

Show Your Child How Cool Certain Foods Are To Eat

The first time a toddler I cared for got a good look at a prickly pineapple, he didn't want anything to do with that weird looking thing! That changed after he watched his mom and dad cut the pineapple open, slice it up and then eat it. That natural curiosity piqued his interest and he just had to try it.

Sometimes even food can be scary to a young child. By eating the food yourself, it can quickly ease their fears if they see you enjoying it first.

Keep It Positive and Fun

It's important not to force your child to eat certain foods. Every parent wants their child to eat a healthy well balanced diet, but some children may be resistant initially. Sometimes a child reacts to how you present the food to them. If you're too forceful and stern, your child will pick up on that and may retaliate by not eating. Or it could simply be that he or she just doesn't like your recipe for green bean soup! It's important not to get upset or punish your child. Remember he or she is learning about new foods, smells, tastes and textures. Allow your child to go at their own pace.

Don't worry, I'm going to help you figure it all out step by step.

Nutrition: Healthy Foods For Your Toddler

You know as a parent the importance of a healthy well balanced diet, even though as adults we don't always eat the way we should. If you want your child to develop good eating habits you're going to have to make some changes. If you're already eating healthy, great. If not, you can't expect your child to eat a healthy diet if he or she is watching you down cheeseburgers and fries every other day.

Your child is going to want to eat what you're eating. Keep this in mind as you move forward. Before you go food shopping here are a few "toddler food facts" you should know.

Toddlers Need Calories!

You may be surprised to learn that pediatricians suggest toddlers should eat between 1,000 and 1,300 calories a day for 2 - 3 year olds and about 900 a day for a toddler at 1 year old. Wow! I know that seems like a lot. Especially with all the news of the increasing number of obese children and those diagnosed with childhood diabetes. A lot of parents are a little freaked out about what their child is eating.

Well, the problem isn't the number of calories. It's the source of those calories. A typical American diet of a hamburger fries and soft drink can easily fulfill that 1,000 calorie requirement at just one meal. Multiply that kind of eating times 4 or 5 and you can see how quickly the calories increase. This can eventually lead to obesity in some children.

So the key is making sure those calories come from quality foods. Quality doesn't have to mean bland veggies either.

Also you don't have to run around with a calculator counting calories. Just make sure your child eats 5 small meals throughout the day. This is roughly 3 meals and 2 snacks. Ideally, you want to aim for 2 servings each of meat, fruit and vegetables a day plus a serving of whole grains with each meal. Also make sure your toddler is drinking at least 2 servings or more of milk each day.

For toddlers under 2, try substituting peanut butter with something easier for them to eat like unsweetened yogurt with fruit.

Here's what a typical day of meals might look like.

Breakfast
- About a cup of whole grain cold or hot cereal. Low or no sugar. Look for cereal with at least 3 grams of fiber.
- Half of a banana sliced
- 1 cup of milk

Snack
- 1 serving of fruit
- Peanut butter on half slice of whole grain bread

Or
- Unsweetened orange juice
- Graham crackers (2)

Lunch
- One slice of whole grain wheat bread cut in half
- A slice of chicken or turkey topped with mustard or a small amount of mayo
- A half a cup of vegetables. Something soft like mashed cauliflower or carrots.
- Milk

Snack 2
- Half an apple or banana. Cut into small pieces. Be sure to remove the skin from the apple.
- Whole grain cereal

Dinner
- Whole wheat pasta. Easy on the sauce. Or whole grain brown rice.
- A half a cup of a soft vegetable
- 1/4 cup of chicken. Cut into small pieces
- 1/2 a cup of milk

Bring On The Fat!

No you didn't misread anything. Toddlers need fat in their diets. See not all fat is bad. In fact, the good fats in foods like peanut butter, milk and whole grains help in the development of your child's central nervous system and brain. During your child's development, good fat is crucial, but just like I mentioned with calories, it's the source of the fat that makes all the difference.

Here's a list of a few "good fats" for toddlers.

- Milk (whole cow's milk)
- Yogurt
- Cheese
- Avocados

Don't Forget About Fiber & Protein

Lean beef, ground turkey and chicken are good sources of protein and iron. Always stick with the lean meats to avoid bad saturated fats.

Eggs are also an excellent source of protein and contain the important Omega-3 essential fatty acids to help your child's brain development and heart health.

Beans not only taste great but also are a good source of fiber and protein plus most kids love eating beans with their fingers! It's fun!

A Word About Juice, Milk and Pre-packaged Foods For Toddlers

It's important to avoid high sugar "fruit drinks" disguised as "fruit juice." This is where you've got to be diligent about reading labels. The majority of fruit drinks are basically sugar flavored water. They contain an enormous amount of sugar. It's not uncommon for an 8 oz serving to have as much as 10 teaspoons of sugar in it. Opt for natural fruit juices without additional artificial sugars added, but keep in mind that even natural fruit juices may have a lot of sugar even without additional sugars being added.

So the rule of thumb is to limit fruit drinks and juices in your toddler's diet.

Too much of anything can be hazardous to the health of your child. You can read more about the affects too much sugar can have on children in the section on How To Handle Sweets.

Milk

If you're a parent opposed to giving your child cow's milk, talk to your child's pediatrician about healthy alternatives. There are other choices including soy milk, almond milk and even rice milk, but it's extremely important to talk to your doctor first.

Consult With Your Child's Pediatrician

Also the diet choices and calories I've mentioned should only be used as a guide. Always consult with your pediatrician before making major changes to your child's diet. Since each child is different, the caloric needs and other nutritional requirements will vary from one child to the next.

Now that you know what to look for, it's time to take a look at the foods in your cupboard. It's okay, I'm going to help you fill your kitchen with delicious nutritious foods for your little one to enjoy.

What's In The Cupboards?

Children are amazing. Watching them grow and learn is so rewarding. They really are like little sponges soaking up lots of information in their little worlds. They learn how to say certain words by listening to other children and adults. They mimic behaviors, sounds and even facial expressions. Pretty much every parent is aware of this and many are careful about saying certain things around young ears. How many times have you spelled a word instead of just saying it? Lots of parents use this tactic in an attempt to to keep their child from knowing about certain things.

When it comes to food choices, many parents don't apply the same rules. Instead it's common for the parent to insist that their child eat lots of vegetables, telling him or her how good they are for them while at the same time scarfing down unhealthy food themselves. That's not to say you have to give up your favorite foods. However, if you want your child to eat and appreciate nutritious foods, you're going to have to lead by example. Think about it. How many times have you offered your child a little bit of whatever you're eating? Eventually it becomes a habit and before you know it your child is always eating whatever you're eating.

If you're not eating a healthy diet, don't expect your child to do so either. If you're already into eating healthy that's awesome. If not, it's time to do some kitchen cupboard food rehab!

The Number One Method To Reduce Junk Food Eating

It's really simple. I call it the "now you see it and now you don't method" of getting rid of bad foods in your kitchen. Most of the time we eat stuff we know we should not on impulse or because we're craving something. Usually this is something sweet, so we keep sugary snack foods around to satisfy those cravings. We also tend to buy things out of habit…things like cookies, potato chips and other comfort foods. If these foods are readily available and in your face, you're going to eat them. So will your child.

By not buying these kinds of foods you can reduce your likelihood of eating them if they're not around. It's also common for a parent to grab a delicious sweet cookie to treat their child or to bribe them in an attempt to control a behavior issue.

In both cases it will lead to a lot of unhealthy eating habits in your child. So focus on not buying bad foods to avoid temptation.

Getting Rid Of Junk Food

Go through your cupboards, refrigerator and freezer. If you've got a lot of cookies and stuff like that, you've got to get rid of them. I've already covered the potential health issues your child can develop from a poor diet. Here's a short list of the foods you should probably get rid of.

- High sugar foods like cookies, cupcakes and candy.
- Foods with high amounts of sodium.
- Fatty foods with high amounts of saturated fats.
- Processed frozen foods targeting young children.

Go Fresh

Freshly prepared foods are always the best option but that may not be an option for working parents. If scheduling is an issue, try preparing meals for your child ahead of time and freezing them. This avoids feeding your child processed frozen foods that are loaded with too much sodium, sugar or bad fats. It's also an easy solution when you're pressed for time.

Restock With Quality Foods

Healthy doesn't have to mean unappetizing. The food industry does a great job at making us believe all those gooey chocolate cupcakes and deep fried foods are great. Let's face it, some of that stuff does taste pretty good! However, that doesn't mean we should indulge to the point of becoming obese and other health problems.

If you want your child to have a healthy lifestyle when they're older you've got to instill good food habits now right from the start. Be careful not to fall into the trap of "Do as I say not as I do" syndrome. Kids are a lot more observant than you think. They will do what you do.

Avoid buying unhealthy foods and opt for better food choices as much as possible. You don't have to run your kitchen like the food police. Just be sensible.

Here are a few items you can include on your next trip to the supermarket.

- Baked chips, pretzels and granola bars.
- Fruit
- Vegetables
- 100% Natural fruit juice (no artificial sugars added)
- Substitute sugary drinks with water as much as possible.
- Whole wheat bread
- Brown rice
- Lean meats - chicken, turkey, lean beef
- Eggs
- Yogurt

Get the idea? Of course your list will vary depending on your own preferences. Choosing healthy is really a lot easier than you think. It's how you prepare the meals that can make a huge difference in how your child adapts.

Take a few minutes to inventory your kitchen. Get rid of the unhealthy foods and create a list of substitutions. Use that as a shopping list. By the way, creating a list before you go shopping increases the chances of you sticking with that list. Try to avoid the habit of getting that unbelievable 10 packs of cookies and cupcakes for $5 deal and opt for fruit instead.

Avoiding sweets can be the biggest hurdle. Next I'll give you some easy strategies you can use to decrease the amount of sweets in your child's diet.

Nanny P

How To Handle Sweets

Depending on who you talk to, sugar is either a wonderful treat or one of the most dangerous ingredients on the planet. Most children, especially those living in Western society, are introduced to sugar right from birth. Many commercially made baby formulas contain sugar. Breast fed babies get sugar in the form of lactose found in their mother's milk.

The Long Term Effects Of Sugar

Too much sugar in your child's diet can lead to tooth decay, excessive weight gain and possible hyperactivity in children diagnosed with ADHD. Although sugar does not cause diabetes, if your family has a history of diabetes, a high sugar diet could be dangerous to your child's health. Also sugar has been found to contribute to heart disease.

What gives sugar a bad rap is the amount in a child's diet. Here's where you can get your toddler off on the right track.

It's almost impossible to completely avoid sugar. I mean it's everywhere and in almost everything we eat and drink. Instead of trying to eliminate it completely from your child's diet, focus on managing it.

Here are a few tips I've found that can work pretty well.

Start Your Toddler With Limited Amounts of Sugar

When children are toddlers, it's a great opportunity to get them used to eating natural foods. How you start out with a child will soon become habits for them. If you're giving your child sweet foods all the time they will develop a taste for even more. The more sugar they eat the more they'll want.

So instead of giving your child that sweetened yogurt, for example, give them the unsweetened yogurt. Add some fresh fruit. If you do it the other way around giving him or her sweetened yogurt and later try to change to unsweetened, I can almost guarantee he or she will not eat it. Once they're "hooked" on sugar it can be very difficult weaning them off.

Establish Some "Sweet Rules" To Help Manage Your Child's Sugar Intake

Decide when, what and how much sweets you'll allow your child to have. For example, a simple rule when it comes to sweets might be to only allow a treat or dessert after dinner. That doesn't mean every single dinner meal should end with a treat, but by establishing a routine your child will learn not to expect sweets except as something special after he or she finishes dinner. You can choose to allow treats at other times instead of dinner…that's up to you. Just be sure to be consistent so your child doesn't get confused.

Give Sweets Every Now And Then As A Treat

If you're giving your toddler a healthy nutritionally balanced diet of fruits, vegetables, fiber, good carbohydrates and proteins, then a sweet dessert every now and then is perfectly fine. Homemade fruit pies without added sugar are always a hit with young children served after a well balanced dinner.

How To Deal With Sugar Outside of Your Home

Sooner or later your toddler is going to get some forbidden candy treat from a neighbor, other kids and grandma and grandpa. It's important to understand and accept that you can't keep your child from getting sugar somewhere else. The best advice I can give you is to be patient and calm. If you catch your child eating candy he or she got from a neighbor or relative, don't make a big deal out of it.

Sit down with your child and explain in a calm manner what your rules are when it comes to eating candy cookies and other sweet treats. Keep it light hearted and tell your child they'll be able to eat the treats after dinner or whenever you decide based on your rules.

If your toddler is in preschool or some kind of day care outside of your home, it would be a good idea to let the provider know about your rules regarding sweets.

Nanny P

Reward Your Child For Trying New Foods

A lot of things we take for granted as adults are new and exciting to a young child. Figuring out how things work and learning about all kinds of new things is how they grow and develop their own personalities.

Trying new foods can be just as much fun. You may assume your child won't like a particular vegetable or fruit. Don't assume the worst. Trying new foods is a process. Some they'll like and others they won't.

Don't Force It

What's most important is that you don't get upset if your child throws a handful of Brussels sprouts across the room with the force of a major league pitcher! Typically this happens if a parent tries to force a child to eat a particular food.

One child I knew got a chance to experience the art and fun of fishing! She was about 6 years old and actually caught a few fish that day. Later that night she watched her mom and dad go through the steps of preparing and cooking the fish but when the fish was placed in front of her on the plate she refused to eat. Puzzled, her mother asked her what was wrong. She looked up at her mom and said "I can't eat a fish I know!"

Instead of forcing the issue her mother made her a nice healthy chicken salad instead.

Reward With Positive Reinforcement

A great approach to having your child try new foods would be to keep the mood upbeat and positive. Smile when introducing a new food. If your child eats it, then come up with a fun way of rewarding their efforts. Nothing over the top, keep it simple.

For example, there was a little girl I cared for who was 3 years old at the time. Each time she did something well or ate something new I would give her a big smile, a thumbs up and say "good job!" every single time. One day after I prepared a tasty fruit smoothie for her, she looked up at me, smiled and gave me thumbs up and a verbal good job!

She had learned to associate a good experience with positive praise. Never punish a child for not eating a certain food. They will begin to associate negative emotions with eating that lead to more severe problems when they're older. Having a nice meal should be a positive experience.

What To Do If Your Child Won't Eat A Certain Food

This one is easy. Let it go. Maybe your child isn't ready for that particular food. It may look strange to him or her. A little boy I knew would take his string beans and carefully open each one and eat the seeds inside, leaving the string bean skin on his plate! This was one of the funniest things ever to watch. Eventually he began to eat the entire bean but he did so when he was ready to do so.

If your child just refuses to try something, remember to keep the mood positive. Try taking a bite yourself and talk about how good it tastes. Then ask if they want to try it too. The majority of the time they'll say yes and give it try.

Another thing to keep in mind is maybe it just doesn't taste good to your child. That may change as they get older or it may not. In the meantime, don't force it. Allow your child to try new foods and reward them with consistent praise when they do.

Toddler Eating Strategies

We've covered the basics of nutrition, shopping, managing sweets and the benefits of rewarding your child for trying out new foods. Next it's time to take a look at a few strategies you can use to deal with some of the most common problems when it comes to getting toddlers to eat.

Here's a list of what's covered next.

- How to get your toddler to eat and enjoy vegetables.
- How you can introduce new foods by taking your child to the supermarket with you.
- Tips for cooking with your toddler and planning menus.
- Making food fun with theme nights and colorful foods!
- Planting a garden with your toddler.

You may find a need for just one of the strategies or all of them. In any case, you'll have a plan you can use whenever you need one.

Nanny P

Strategy 1: Getting Sneaky With Veggies

The US government concluded after a study conducted in 2011 that only about 22% of children between the ages of 2 and 5 were getting the recommended amount of vegetables in their diet. According to the study, half of a child's plate should be fruits and vegetables. Unfortunately, most children were getting their veggies from potato chips and deep fried fries.

So How Do You Get Toddlers to Eat Their Veggies?

As soon as toddlers are safely able to eat soft veggies they should be a part of their regular meals every day at every meal if possible. This is an excellent way to get them used to eating healthy vegetables right from the start.

If you wait until they're older to begin giving them vegetables, you may find it is a lot more difficult to get them to try new foods. As kids get older they begin to form their own likes and dislikes about a lot of different things especially food.

Is It Okay To Use Sneaky Tactics?

I don't think there's anything wrong with being a little sneaky when it comes to kids and eating healthy. Often times kids will refuse to eat something because they have somehow gotten it into their heads that whatever it is it's just not going to taste good. I've found that this happens a lot when a parent goes into lecture mode about eating vegetables. The demeanor is usually stern and a young child associates eating vegetables as not being fun.

Think about it. Chances are when you were a child and your parents gave you something sweet to eat, it was done in a positive light hearted manner. Right away you associated positive feelings with sweets.

So using different strategies to get your toddler to feel good about eating vegetables is fine.

Here are a few you can try with your little one.

Create Fun Stories

If you've ever seen one of those old Popeye The Sailor cartoons there was always a consistent theme. He would always say that he got his muscles because he ate his spinach. Creating a game or story that ends with a great benefit to the child if they eat their vegetables can work very well.

"Eat your spinach because it's good for you" doesn't have the same effect as something a toddler can better relate to. If he or she has a favorite cartoon character, find a way to include that character into your story.

"Hey did you know Dora the Explorer loves to eat spinach just like you?...It makes her happy and soon she'll be a big girl just like you one day!"

If your child wants to be a fireman or firewoman when they grow up, use that to your advantage. Tell them how eating his or her spinach will help make them great fire fighters!

Hungry Enough To Eat…A Plate Full of Veggies!

Once you get a good idea of what your child likes the most, have an all veggie meal. It's a great way to introduce new veggies as well. When a child is hungry, that plate of vegetables is going look really good. You may find very little protesting and more requests for second helpings.

Get Creative With The Menu

Find recipes for vegetables that are both healthy and delicious. Take cauliflower for example. Some children aren't too interested in eating it. It looks odd and can be a little bland. Take that same cauliflower and mash it up and it looks a lot like mashed potatoes. Add low fat cream cheese.

Tasty!

Strategy 2: Getting The Kids Involved With Grocery Shopping

Coming up with creative ways to get your child to eat healthy foods can be a challenge at times. In addition to the ideas I shared in the previous section, you can make your child feel more involved when it comes to choosing new foods.

Pack Up The Kids, Crank Up The Car and Head To The Supermarket!

A great way to get your child to try new healthy food choices is to take them with you the next time you go grocery shopping. Taking your child to the grocery store may not be anything new, but what you do with your child this time probably will be.

Instead of having your child watch you shop for groceries, let him or her help pick out new foods to try. Of course you will need to steer clear of the dreaded potato chips and cookies aisle. Park yourself in the produce section and pick out a couple of new vegetables to try. Let your child hold it. Encourage your son or daughter to smell it.

Keep the mood fun and lighthearted. After a few minutes, smile and ask your child if he or she thinks you should give it a try for dinner. If they say yes, be excited and thank your child for helping you pick out dinner.

If your child says no, you can either try your luck with another vegetable or try again another time. You can let your child know how helpful they are and you would like them to help you pick out food again the next time.

Set The Stage

Children love pretending to be just like mommy and daddy. So before you schedule your grocery store shopping day, pick up one of those toddler sized grocery carts. Let your child shop alongside you in the store.

When you find the new vegetable, fruit or other healthy choices, try to place it in your child's cart. They will really get a kick out of the whole thing. It will also make them feel they are really helping you shop for food. It may also make introducing new foods a little easier.

Go Organic

When buying fresh vegetables and fruits, I recommend buying organic. The amount of pesticides used on foods and growth hormones in meat aren't healthy for young children.

Strategy 3: Getting The Kids Involved With Cooking

Getting your children involved with cooking is another way to get them interested in trying out new foods and flavors. However, before you begin there are a few things to keep in mind in terms of safety and age appropriate activities.

Safety Comes First

Keep sharp objects beyond your child's reach.
Make sure things like cleaning supplies are stored away safely. Purchase child safety locks for the refrigerator and any cupboards low enough for your child to open. You can find them at any hardware store. They're inexpensive and easy to install.

Cooking Activities For Toddlers 1 - 2 Years

Very young toddlers won't be able to do much in the kitchen when you're cooking, but that doesn't mean they can't participate.

Place your child in a high chair so they can see what you're doing as you cook. Make a game out of the process. Sing the names of fruits and vegetables you're preparing. Or if you're cooking chicken for example, teach your child the sounds a chicken makes.

Talk about what you're doing as you cook. Don't be concerned with the fact they have no idea what you're talking about. At this age, they are taking it all in. You'll be very surprised when he or she is able to tell you out of the blue that the vegetable you're holding is a carrot!

You can also do other things like letting them feel what the flour feels like or the bread.

Toddlers 2 - 3 Years

Kids love to be mom or dad's little helper. There are a few safe, easy and fun jobs your child can do to help you prepare the family meal.

It's perfectly fine to let your child help stir ingredients or even add them to a food processor for you. Just make sure you are supervising each step to make sure your child is always safe. If you're introducing new fruits for example, you could let your child decide which fruit should be cut first or added to a blender.

You could let your child be the one to push the button to start the blender. You'll find your child is eager to help and may be more open to trying the new food because he or she helped to make it.

The more you allow your child to help you in the kitchen, the more he or she may become curious about the different foods you're preparing. Don't worry if your child still won't try new foods. Give it time and eventually they'll come around.

Strategy 4: Create Theme Nights

Planning theme nights once a week is another way to get kids to try new foods. It's also a great way to bond and create some awesome memories.

Choosing A Theme

There are no rules to choosing a theme. Since the goal is to get your child to try new foods, come up with a list of possible ideas. Here are a few to get you started.

You can choose different ethnic menus for themes.

Mexican
Italian
Asian
Caribbean

Feel free to get even more creative.

How about breakfast for dinner night!
All veggies and fruit day!
Chicken Wednesdays
New Food Fridays!

Well you get the idea. Making new foods fun can help reduce the stress young children tend to feel when they're learning about new things.

The ideas I've given you here is just to give you a starting point. You'll come up with a lot of new fun ideas on your own and I'd love to hear what you come up with.

Go Shopping

Here's another opportunity to take your child shopping and allow them to help you choose the ingredients and various foods for the theme you've chosen. You don't have to prepare a 7 course meal. It's perfectly fine and easier to just pick one item. Maybe dessert, a vegetable, or protein.

Make It Festive

You want your child to associate trying new foods with a fun positive experience. So have fun. Play some Italian music on Italian night for example. Dance with your child. Even if he or she doesn't end up liking the food, your child will be open to trying new foods the next theme night because it was so much fun.

Strategy 5: Planning Menus Together

Planning menus with a toddler can be fun for you and your child. Now of course a very young child can't possibly participate in any complicated planning. However, you can let your child choose the vegetable, fruit or protein for the meal. Encourage him or her to choose one of their favorites and then choose something new to go along to include in the dish.

How To Help Your Toddler Choose

Use pictures of foods your child may be familiar with. Look for color photos of different foods in food magazines. Cut them out and divide them into different food groups. Even if your child has no idea what they're looking at that's okay. They will enjoy being a part of the decision making process. It makes them feel important.

You can make a game out of it by letting them choose a vegetable to include. Or have them choose a protein or fruit for dessert.

Flashcards

You can also use flashcards with pictures of foods. It may also help them to learn the names of foods and learn more about the foods they like and don't like.

Take The Pictures To The Grocery Store

You can create your menu and list of ingredients. Take the pictures of the different foods chosen by your toddler and head to the grocery store. Again, make it fun to look for new foods. In this case look for the vegetables, fruits or proteins that match the picture he or she chose.

Remember to keep the mood fun. Your toddler will look forward to helping you plan menus and play "find the food" games at the grocery store.

Nanny P

Strategy 6: Choosing Foods of Certain Colors

If you want to know how creating a plate full of colorful foods can be a great way to get your child to try new foods, just take a look at some of their favorite toys. Many of their toys are made of bright colors. They're visually appealing and toddlers are drawn to them.

So doing the same with their food may spark enough curiosity to get your child at least interested in trying out new foods. You could encourage your child to choose his or her favorite colors then later you can work on adding in other colorful fruits and veggies. From a health perspective, the more colorful the better.

Here's a run down of some colorful foods to include on your next shopping trip. I've also included a little bit of information on the health benefits of each group.

Green Things!
Some members of the green family contain lutein which can help maintain good eye health. Lutein rich green foods include:

Spinach
Green peppers
Peas
Cucumber
Celery

Other green veggies and fruits may help protect against certain cancers. They include:

Green Beans
Green apples
Avocado
Asparagus
Broccoli
Green grapes
Green onions
Kiwi
Honeydew melon

Lettuce
Zucchini

Yellow & Orange Super Heroes!
This food group contains carotenoids that occur naturally in the pigment of fruits and vegetables that may decrease the chance of getting some cancers, strengthen the immune system and reduce the risk of heart disease. Here are a few fruits and veggies to consider.

Squash
Carrots
Sweet potatoes
Sweet corn
Yellow Peppers
Yellow Tomatoes
Oranges
Pumpkins
Pineapple
Pears
Peaches
Lemons
Apricots
Mangoes
Tangerines

Red Fruits and Vegetables
Red fruits and vegetables contain lycopene or anthocyanins. Lycopene is believed to reduce the risk of certain cancers while foods containing anthocyanins are known to prevent cell damage and are also good for heart health.

Tomatoes
Red peppers
Beets
Rhubarb
Red Potatoes
Radishes
Pink grapefruit
Raspberries

Pomegranates
Red grapes
Cherries
Strawberries
Watermelon

Blue/Purple
Blue/Purple foods are antioxidants that protect cell damage and may also prevent heart disease, some cancers and strokes.

Purple grapes
Blueberries
Blackberries
Prunes
Raisins
Eggplant

White Veggies & Fruit
White veggies & fruit like other more colorful fruits and vegetables also contain anthocyanins. Some also have allicin which can keep cholesterol and blood pressure in check.

Cauliflower
Mushrooms
Onions
Turnips

Potatoes
Bananas (Both provide potassium)

There are several other fruits and vegetables you can include but this should be enough to spark some ideas for meal planning.

Nanny P

Strategy 7: Starting A Garden

If you're the "nature type" and you want to pass it on to your child, consider starting a garden if you have the means to do so. Growing your own food can be healthy and educational for your child.

Your child can learn about how fruits and vegetables grow by helping you dig the holes, dropping in the seeds and helping you keep the garden well watered.

When it's time to pick from the garden, you can let your child help you choose which ones to they would like to try. Then you can let them help you prepare the foods for meals.

You can pick up books on starting your own garden at your local library or bookstore.

Nanny P

A Word About Good Table Manners

It can be fun for both you and your child to learn about eating delicious fruits, vegetables and enjoying new recipes. However, it's also important to teach toddlers how they should act while food is being served. It's never too early to begin teaching basic rules on how to behave at the table at home or out in public at a restaurant.

If you've ever been to a restaurant and had to endure young children running up and down the aisles, throwing food and simply behaving badly, you already know how frustrating that can be. It's not the child's fault. Blame the parents. If a child isn't being taught good table manners at home, don't expect them to be on their best behavior out in public.

It's the responsibility of the parents to take the time to teach their children how to behave at the table. It's best to start the training early. Kids can develop both good and bad habits fairly quickly.

Start While They're Young

It will take your child awhile to put the pieces together in terms of learning good table manners, so don't expect him or her to get it right away. Your child will learn over time at his or her own pace.

Create A Routine

I can't stress the importance of developing routines for young children. They learn from repetition. Routines also help children feel more confident when they know what to expect.

Here's an example of a very simple but effective routine.

Have your toddler wash their hands right before every meal. You will have to assist them of course. You are establishing a new habit for your child.

Once you place your child in their high chair, you can teach them that throwing their spoon or food and other behavior you decide is not proper won't be allowed.

Or if they're not in a high chair, you need to teach your child that running around disturbing others while they are eating is not appropriate.

You need to correct bad behavior every single time. That doesn't mean physically punishing or yelling at your child. It simply means corrected the behavior by showing your child what the appropriate behavior should be.

How To Deal With Bad Behavior During Meal Time

One method is to ignore the bad behavior. Some children "act out" in order to get attention. When they finally realize their tactics aren't working, the bad behavior either stops completely or lessens quite a bit.

Another way to deal with bad manners is to always remain calm and simply remove your child from the table each time he or she acts inappropriately. Let them know they cannot do certain things when it's time to sit down and eat. Eventually your child will put two and two together. He or she will learn that in order to eat with everyone else they have to act appropriately.

Every child has their own personality and no one knows them better than you do. You may have to find ways to use that to your advantage to get your child to behave accordingly.

Reward Good Behavior With Gentle Praise

When your child obeys the rules give him or her praise. Nothing over the top…just a simple "good job" and a smile is enough. They want to please you. Seeing your smiling face and and hearing a reassuring tone of voice is a big deal for young children. Just make sure you don't give too much praise. Otherwise your child may associate praise with meal time. You don't want your child thinking the most important thing is getting big praise and attention every time he or she sits down to eat. So just keep it calm give a little praise and move on.

What Can You Teach A Toddler?

Even if your child isn't talking yet, they're listening to everything around them. Their little brains are always trying to figure out what's going on in their environment. Saying "please and thank you" whenever appropriate will teach your child the importance of saying these words when asking for something or receiving something. They also learn by imitating what you do, so make sure you're using good table manners. Your child will eventually get it and begin to follow your example.

Don't Force Your Child To Finish Everything On Their Plate

Let your child decide when he or she has had enough. Just because you put food on the plate doesn't mean your child will be able to eat it all. When they're full, they're done. Forcing them to eat can create negative associations about food later in life.

Very young children can't verbalize they've had enough to eat and will find other ways to get their point across to you.

A full and bored toddler will begin to play with their food. This might include throwing their food, building mini forts on their plate or seeing how much they can feed to the family dog!

Recognize your child has had enough to eat and remove them from the table.

How To Avoid Restaurant Meltdowns

Unfortunately toddlers will wait until they get out in public to completely forget about all that wonderful home training. New environments with lots of strange people, sounds and other distractions can create stress in children. Add hunger into the mix and you've got a recipe for embarrassment and some pretty annoyed restaurant guests.

There's no way to predict what your little angel will do. Take a quiet toy with you to the restaurant. Something that will keep your child's attention without disturbing other guests. It's difficult for young children to sit still for long periods of time. Having a favorite toy may help keep your child calm.

If your child ends up acting out, don't get angry and start yelling. Remind him or her about acting appropriately. If the behavior gets to the point where people are beginning to give you the "eye roll of discontent" consider asking for a doggie bag and heading home.

With practice and time your child will learn how to behave in public so continue to be consistent with correcting behavior. Eventually your child will settle down and act appropriately. Be sure to check out the Resources section of this book for a list of great books on teaching your toddler good manners.

Get Started!

You now have some easy strategies you can use to get your child to discover new foods and enjoy eating a healthy diet. After reading the strategy sections you've probably already come up with some additional ideas of your own. That's great! Follow your instincts and move forward. If one strategy doesn't work try something else or combined strategies. Eventually you'll find one that works very well for your child.

Don't worry about making mistakes, just start again and you will figure it out.

Bon Appetit!

Nanny P

Resources

Excuse Me! A Little Book of Manners - Karen Katz
http://www.amazon.com/dp/0448425858/

Ages - 2 and up

This is a beautifully written and simple way to teach your little boy or girl their manners. Karen Katz does an excellent job of teaching young children when to say excuse me, thank you, I'm sorry and more. It's an interactive lift the flap book so your child can learn by looking at pictures and hearing the words from you.

The Baby and Toddler Cookbook: Fresh, Homemade Foods for a Healthy Start - Karen Ansel
http://www.amazon.com/dp/1740899806/

Preparing healthy meals for your toddler without all of the added sugar and other harmful ingredients is easy if you cook them yourself. This book has several fantastic meals you can prepare for your child that are delicious and healthy.

Roots, Shoots, Buckets & Boots: Gardening Together with Children - Sharon Lovejoy
http://www.amazon.com/dp/0761110569/

This is a favorite and highly rated book to help you and your child enjoy gardening together. What a fantastic way to introduce new foods to a child. He or she will learn how their favorite fruits and vegetables grow while helping you plant them in their very own garden.

Nanny P

Nanny Notes on Toddlers

Nanny P's
Blueprint For
Getting Your Toddler to Sleep

Nanny P

Nanny P's Blueprint for Getting Your Toddler to Sleep

Nanny P

Starting Off With The Right Mindset: Prepare Yourself First

It can be really frustrating dealing with an energetic toddler all day long. Night time comes and all you want to do is settle down and get some rest. Unfortunately your child will often have other plans and going to sleep is not on their list!

Patience and calm has to be your response. Try to remember your child is taking in everything in their environment. Playing, eating and discovering new things gets to be a lot of fun. Going to sleep just doesn't seem like a good idea to them yet. So as a parent, it will be up to you to manage your toddler's "social schedule" and provide the right kind of structure to make sure your toddler gets plenty of rest.

What To Expect From This Book

In the following sections I will give you a step by step plan to create a bedtime sleep routine for your toddler. Plus you'll also learn how eating certain foods are not only healthy they can also get your child to sleep faster. I'll give you easy to follow methods you can begin using today to deal with bed wetting, nightmares, breastfeeding and several other tips and issues to get your toddler to go to sleep.

So, let's get started. Bedtime will be here before you know it!

Nanny P

How Much Sleep Does Your Child Need?

If most toddlers could communicate the way most adults can, they would probably tell us that sleeping is way overrated! They've got too many toys, fun and exploring to do, who needs sleep?

Well, toddlers need a huge amount of sleep. Their brains and immune systems need the body to sleep in order to function properly. Everything your child learns when awake gets processed further by their brain during sleep. Plus growth hormones are also released while your child is sleeping.

How Much Sleep Does A Toddler Really Need?

Most pediatricians and others involved in child development suggest toddlers between the ages of 1 and 3 years should get 10 - 14 hours of sleep a day. However, most toddlers for a variety of reasons average on the lower end of 10 hours a day. This includes regular night time hours and naps during the day.

Lack of Sleep Can Cause Some Problems

When small children don't get enough sleep it can lead to behavioral problems. Have you felt darn right cranky at work because you didn't get enough sleep the night before? Well your child goes through almost the same feelings. Irritability and stress can be the result if your child isn't getting enough sleep.

Nanny P

Putting All The Pieces Together

Getting a toddler to sleep in a healthy positive environment is the most important thing to keep in mind as you read through this book. This means creating a bedtime routine for your child. The best routines involve more than just putting your child to bed at the same time every night.

In the next sections, I'll give you some easy tips to help you create a great bedtime routine for your child.

Here's what you'll learn:

How the right foods and exercise can actually help your child fall asleep.

The importance of napping.

The kinds of activities that will keep your child awake for hours and how to avoid them.

Why toddlers must have consistency when it comes to sleeping.

How to create a near perfect bedtime routine.

Tips to make your child's room sleep friendly.

Grab a pen and paper to take notes. Chances are you'll come up with some creative ideas of your own.

Nanny P

Tip 1: Nutrition and Exercise

It should go without saying that proper nutrition and exercise play a major role in developing sound sleep patterns in children. However, many parents are unaware of the effects that some foods can have on children. Also most think their child is getting enough exercise just from playing all day.

Let's first take a look at how nutrition can help your child to get a good night of sleep. Just as adults need to eat a healthy balanced diet so do young children. Also certain kinds of foods can actually help toddlers sleep better at night like a healthy carbohydrate and some protein as an example.

Certain complex carbohydrates contain tryptophan which causes one to feel sleepy. Tryptophan is an amino acid that occurs naturally in certain foods and is not harmful to your child. It also plays a major role in the growth of children. The human body cannot manufacture tryptophan so we need to eat foods that contain it.

The protein part of the snack is to control hunger so he or she isn't up in the middle of the night wanting food.

Bedtime Toddler Snacks With Tryptophan & Protein
- Cheese
- Milk
- Eggs
- Soy Milk
- Cottage cheese
- Nuts (Only for older toddlers over the age of 3)
- Turkey
- Tofu

Carbohydrates For Toddlers
- Whole grain cereal
- Oatmeal cookie
- Apple (slice)
- Peanut butter on a slice of whole grain bread if your toddler is 3 and older. Or peanut butter on an apple slice.

Exercise

Believe it or not, all of that running around all day is not exactly considered exercise. In addition to play time activities, your child should also engage in some kind of structured exercise everyday for about 30 minutes.

It can be something as simple as playing ball with your child, getting him or her to run, jump, throw and kick. Or riding a tricycle or other toy that requires them to pedal or scoot around in order to get from point A to point B. You can also opt for a 30 minute walk to the park.

Toddlers need to burn off the energy from the day so they can settle down at bedtime. Getting lots of exercise will wear them down so they can relax and allow their body to prepare for sleep.

Not only will your child sleep better but he or she will develop good habits and attitudes toward exercise. However, kids learn by watching you so if you're spending several hours in front of the television and not getting any structured exercise yourself, remember your child will do as you do.

Tip 2: Napping

Toddlers take naps because their bodies are growing. That may seem pretty simple but the thing is that the growth process demands a lot of energy. The food your child eats is the energy source their little body uses to keep the various processes churning right along.

When their body runs out of energy, they get sleepy and take a nap. Toddlers have a lot going on in their little worlds. Napping also allows their brains to process information and their bodies to rest. During sleep their body can recharge itself to carry on the rest of the day.

Napping changes as a child gets older because they require less sleep.

Typical Toddler Napping

Every child is different so please look at the napping schedules only as a guide. Observe your child's pattern. You'll be able to get a better idea of when nap time is most appropriate.

Generally by the time a child reaches a year, they should get 14 hours of sleep a day. Aim for 11 of those hours at bedtime. The remaining 3 hours should be nap time. You can try scheduling naps twice a day.

Toddler Napping Age 2 - 3 Years

On average toddlers in this age range should get at least 11 hours of sleep at night and at least an hour to two hours of nap time during the day. By the time your child reaches 2 or 3 years old they will naturally go from napping twice a day to just one.

Nothing Is Set In Stone

Although from a health point of view, your child should get the suggested amount of sleep, it is likely your child may not sleep as long or nap as much. You will have to experiment and observe your child's sleeping patterns. You will be the best judge as to when your toddler is most likely to take a nap.

Nanny P

Tip 3: Avoiding Stimulation Before Bed

When it's getting close to bedtime there are a few things you should try to avoid before putting your child to sleep for the night.

Some of the most common foods, drinks and activities can keep your child from falling asleep. Here are a few of the most common stimulates almost guaranteed to make your nights as sleepless as possible!

Caffeine

I think it's safe to assume you're not giving your child coffee so no worries about that as a source of caffeine. There are other foods that contain caffeine to avoid. They include dark chocolate, hot cocoa and some processed foods may contain caffeine. Make sure you read labels carefully.

Too Many Naps

This is a tough one. I've seen parents wake their kids up from naps if they feel the child has been sleeping too long. The point of course is they don't want the child up all night. However, when a child sleeps for longer periods of time it usually means their body needs the rest.

If your child's pediatrician can find no medical reason for it then you'll have to spend some time managing your child's naps. Try getting your child to nap earlier in the day and make sure you do so at the same time each day.

Television

Watching television right before going to bed is an easy way to get your child over stimulated and awake for several hours. Television is visually stimulating. Plus let's face it, some of the stuff that ends up on television can be pretty gross and scary for a toddler.

Imagine being sent to bed with all those scary images in your head. Sleeping is the last thing you would want to do so imagine it from the perspective of a young child. Limit the amount of television your child watches throughout the day and especially an hour or two before bed.

If you do allow your toddler to watch television choose something that's more laid back and avoid the scary stuff. You could buy lullaby CDs or toddler targeted stories on DVD that they can watch instead of regular television.

Horseplay

If you have older children, consider making some rules about too much rough housing close to bedtime. Children love to have fun, chasing each other and wrestling. These kinds of activities are way too stimulating and will keep your child alert and wide awake.

Tip 4: Consistent Bedtime

When it comes to toddlers and children in general, consistency is one of the most important things you must be aware of in order to get your child to sleep. Children need to feel secure about themselves and their surroundings.

They can get that feeling from always expecting things to be done a certain way all the time. It also reduces stress. Anytime a young child is introduced to a new way of doing things it can cause a certain amount of insecurity and stress. You can help alleviate their stress by always being consistent so they can always know what to expect and what's expected of them.

Bedtime

Part of your toddler sleeping plan should include a specific bedtime. Since toddlers need at least 11 hours of sleep at night, getting them to bed by 7:30 p.m. should be reasonable for most. That's not set in stone. You are the one who will decide the best bedtime for your child.

One way to do that is to observe when your child tends to get sleepy at night. If you notice a pattern around the same time each night, then choose that time for bedtime. You also want to avoid sending him or her to bed too early, so experiment a bit to see what works best.

Set The Time

Once you've decided on the best time, stick with it. That means every night your toddler should be headed for bed at the same time no matter what. In addition to setting a specific time, you'll need to factor in extra time before your child actually goes to bed. It's a bedtime routine that should begin about an hour before sleep time.

In the next section I'll give you some ideas on how to set up your own bedtime routine.

Nanny P

Tip 5: Routine Before Bed

The Key To A Sleeping Toddler...Establish a Routine

Establishing a bedtime routine for your toddler is very important. If you've read my other books on getting toddlers to eat and potty training then you're already aware of the positive results you can achieve, when you create and maintain a routine.

When a child gets used to doing something the same way over and over again it helps them build confidence. It also makes them feel more secure. On the other hand, when there are no rules they can become cranky, frustrated and their behavior can really get out of hand.

How To Set Up A Sleep Routine For Your Child

First, you'll need to come up with a plan. That means deciding what will be included in your bedtime routine.

Here's a list of ideas:
- Warm baths
- Bedtime snack
- Reading a story
- Associate a specific task that is always done before bedtime. This could be spending time putting toys away or choosing which pajamas to wear for the night.
- Sleeping with a favorite toy

Now from the sample list above, here's how a basic sleep routine plan might work.

Just before bedtime have your child help you pick up all of their toys around the house. Place them in a designated room, area or play box. Soon your child will associate putting away the toys with getting ready for bed.

While putting away toys you can verbally let your child know that it's time to get ready for bed. You keep the mood light hearted but not so much that your child thinks it's a game he or she can choose not to play. So while your demeanor should remain calm, your tone should let your child know play time is over.

Next prepare a nice warm bath for your child. Not only will you have a nice clean little one but there's also another reason. The bath will raise your child's body temperature just enough to make him or her sleepy. It's also a great way to help your child wind down and relax.

After the bath, change him or her into their pajamas and then offer a small snack before bedtime. Don't forget to brush your son or daughter's teeth after snacking on a healthy carbohydrate and some protein. (You can get some food ideas in the Nutrition and Exercise section)

Read a story from one of your child's favorite books.

Lights out and goodnight.

Tip 6: A Nice Sleeping Environment

Take some time to create a pleasant sleeping environment for your child. Every child is different so I've put together a list of ideas you may want to consider.

Relaxing Music - This is where those lullaby CDs can come in handy.

Night Light - If your child is afraid of the dark, a night light will usually help them calm down.

Sleep Clocks - I included a lot more detail about using sleep clocks in the Early Risers section. They can be wonderful tools when it comes to teaching toddlers about sleeping and when it's okay to get out of bed the next morning.

White Noise - Many parents use white noise to help children sleep better. You can get the same effect using a regular house fan but your child's room will end up being a bit chilly.

Quiet Toys - Make sure the toys you do allow at bedtime are quiet and aren't too distracting. A favorite stuffed animal, doll or small toy car should be fine.

Nanny P

Dealing With Toddler Sleep Issues

At this point you should have a bedtime routine planned and ready to start with your child. If you're still working on one, that's fine. It's better to take a little more time if needed to create a routine that both you and your child can stick with.

Once you begin working with your child and the new bedtime routine, I can almost guarantee you're going to run into some common road blocks every parent ends up having to deal with. So I've included 6 of the most common issues when it comes to getting your child to sleep and how to deal with each.

The issues covered include:

What to do when your toddler refuses to go to bed.

How to stop your child from wanting to sleep in your bed instead of their own.

A few methods you can use to make sure your child sleeps through the night.

How to handle bed wetting at night.

Sharing a room with a sibling.

How to teach your child not to wake you up at 5 a.m.!

Chances are one or more of the above issues is either a problem now or will be soon enough…just trust me on this one! If one of the issues is a big problem right now, feel free to skip to that specific issue. You can always go back and read the others later.

Now, let's get started.

Nanny P

Issue 1: Not Wanting to go to Bed

If there's one thing every parent will have to deal with sooner or later, it's the day your toddler decides he or she is not going to bed! There can be any number of reasons why your child decides going to sleep is not a part of their plan. The best way to deal with this issue is to try and figure out why your child refuses to go to bed in the first place.

Here are a few of the most common reasons and how to deal with each.

Having Too Much Fun - This is covered in more detailed in the section on avoiding stimulation before bed. Young children love to be a part of whatever is going on so they protest when you remove them from the fun.

Avoid too much high energy activity, television and play within one hour of bed. Start the winding down process at least an hour before bedtime. Include this period as a part of your child's bedtime routine.

There's A Monster In The Closet! - Or under the bed or somewhere in their room. A child can be genuinely frightened by a toy placed in a chair at the foot of his bed for example. During the day it's just another toy but at night it takes on a life of its own.

Very young children can't use logic to figure out it's just the chair casting a shadow or that scary sound is a loose shutter. You can try to reassure your child that there's no monster in their room but usually that won't convince them.

So you can give your child some ways to "protect" themselves from the monsters in their room. Maybe get under the covers and close their eyes and soon they will just go away.

Another way that may be effective is to give your child some special "monster repellent" that scares all the monsters under the bed and in the closet away.

A simple plastic water bottle is all you need. Tell your child if they see the monster just spray him and it will scare that ole monster away. For children who are afraid of the dark a night light usually does the trick.

Bad Dreams - Comfort your child by hugging him or her and letting them know everything is fine now and there's no need to be afraid. Another idea is to give your child a "bad dream" distraction.

Tell him or her that if they have the dream again, just hold on to their favorite stuffed toy and hug it really tight. Tell him or her that you have given their special toy lots of extra love to take care of them at night so they don't have to be afraid again.

Try to remind them about something funny that happened to get their mind off the bad dream. You can also tell them what you do when you feel scared. Maybe you close your eyes and laugh until you get sleepy again. It will make your child feel a lot better knowing that even mommies and daddies get scared too.

Separation Anxiety - For some children being separated from their parents is frightening. Add being placed in a dark room alone and their anxiety level can go through the roof. Just reassure your child that it's okay to go to sleep and you'll be there when they wake up the next morning. Do so in a matter of fact tone and don't make a big deal out it.

How To Get Your Child To Go To Bed

First, it's really important that you stick to the bedtime routine you've created for your child. No matter how much your child protests don't give in.

Second, if your child begins to cry it's perfectly fine to comfort him or her but limit it to a couple of minutes to get your child to calm down. If the crying continues go back every few minutes until the crying stops or they drift off to sleep. If the next night you have the same problem, rinse and repeat except this time you're going to wait a few minutes longer than you did the previous night.

For example, on the first night wait about 2 - 3 minutes before going to your child's room to calm him or her down. Then the next night, wait 3 - 5 minutes. Give your child reassurance that they will be fine and you'll be there to wake them up the next morning. Leave the room. If your child cries wait 3-5 minutes before going back again. Keep this up until they fall asleep.

Eventually as the time gets longer and longer your child will begin to feel more and more secure.

Let Your Toddler Share In The Routine

You can also try getting your toddler to help you with their sleep routine. As you go about each step ask your toddler what comes next. Make going to bed a positive experience.

Rewards

A very effective method in potty training is the use of stickers as rewards. Giving rewards also works really well with sleep training. Little ones love stickers. You can tell your child that if he or she goes to bed there will be a nice new sticker for them in the morning.

If All Else Fails Don't Do Anything At All

If the above methods don't work then you'll have to have a tough skin and allow your child to cry it out. Children learn very quickly what to do to get your attention. Some stop talking or obeying. Others throw temper tantrums while others cry. If you give in to your child every time he or she cries you're teaching them how to control you.

It may be tough to do, but do not go into your child's room if they insist on crying for an extended period of time. Eventually, he or she will either get tired and fall asleep or they will figure out that crying to get out of bed isn't working and will stop the behavior. It may take a few nights of crying before your child figures it out so be prepared.

Nanny P

Issue 2: Wanting to Sleep with Parents

Toddlers everywhere at one time or another will end up sleeping with their parents. In the beginning it's cute and everyone ends up getting a great night of sleep. Eventually, as a parent you reach a point when you decide your toddler needs to sleep in their own bed.

How you will handle and change this behavior will depend on how long your child has been sleeping with you. Some children have spent almost their entire young lives sleeping with mommy and daddy. Others may do so only whenever they feel like it.

How To Get Your Toddler To Sleep In Their Own Bed

In this case you're going to have to wean your child from sleeping in your bed. The best route to take is to do so gradually.

Make sure you keep the mood upbeat and positive. You can tell your child that big boys and girls get to sleep in their own room and in their own beds. YAY! If you've used the sticker rewards and your child responds well to them, then use the same technique when getting your child to sleep in their own bed.

Another method is to work on transitioning them to sleeping on their own over several nights. Place your child in their bed and stay in the room with them until they fall asleep. Then every 2 - 3 nights move your physical location a little further away. So if you start off sitting on the edge of their bed the first couple of nights then switch to a chair. Keep moving towards the door every 2 - 3 nights until you're finally out of the room completely.

Try not to stay in the same location for more than 3 days. Otherwise your child may get used to you being in that position and may begin to get anxious if suddenly after a week you're no longer where they're used to seeing you.

Always remember to praise your child for sleeping on their own. Soon they'll get used to sleeping in their own room and you can reclaim your bed.

If you have a child that is already sleeping in their own bed but occasionally wants to sleep in your bed you can choose to allow it from time to time or not. It's really up to you. If you don't want your child sleeping in your bed then be consistent about not allowing it. If your child isn't sleeping through the night and is waking you up, the next section will help you manage your child's sleeping habits.

Issue 3: Not Sleeping Through The Night

Just when you thought it was safe to get in your favorite sleeping position you hear something you've heard a thousand times:

"Mom…Dad I can't sleep. There's a monster in my room!"

"Is it time to get up now?"

"Can I sleep in the bed with you mommy?"

The reason your child wakes up in the middle of the night is because they haven't learned how to go back to sleep on their own yet. Actually, it's human nature that both children and adults awake in the middle of the night almost nightly. Even if you don't have any memory of doing so it happens. Mainly because as an adult you've learned how to naturally turn over and go right back to sleep.

Most toddler experience of getting to sleep happens with the help of a parent. Other things can cause your child to have problems sleeping through the night. Remember those monsters under the bed? They're back! Don't forget about nightmares! When a child is afraid of something the first thing they want is to feel safe and confident those monsters can't get to them. The safest place to a child is wherever you are.

How To Get Your Child To Sleep Through The Night

Like anything else, this is a process that will take as long as it takes for your child to change. It's important that you do not punish your child for waking you up in the middle of the night. Always stay calm.

If your child wanders into your room at 2 a.m. get up and take him or her back to their own room. Tuck your child back in bed, give a kiss and say goodnight. If your child gets up again repeat.

This may go on for quite some time until your child falls asleep again. You should also be prepared to keep doing this for several nights until your child finally stops. If you stay consistent you'll get the desired result.

You may also use some of the methods described in the section Not Wanting To Go To Bed to get your child to go back to sleep in their own bed.

If your child isn't feeling well, it's a judgment call on your part as to whether or not to make an exception to your bedtime rules.

Issue 4: Bed Wetting

How To Deal With Bed Wetting At Night

Most young children will have issues wetting the bed at night until 5 years of age. When children wet the bed at night even if they've been potty trained it's because they're just not physically ready yet.

It's going to take time for them to get to the point where they can avoid wetting the bed at night. For now you have to be aware that their bladders are small. There is also a certain amount of muscle control needed to keep from having an accident.

Unfortunately, those muscles aren't strong enough to stop your child from wetting the bed. When older children and adults have to go to the bathroom in the middle of the night they get a physical urge that signals to get up and go. Toddlers tend to sleep so soundly they don't feel this urge and that's how accidents happen.

Potty Trained Toddlers

Since toddlers lack the physical ability to avoid wetting the bed at night even if they are potty trained, the best way to deal with it is to have them wear either diapers at night or training pants. Most toddlers won't have consistently dry nights for 3 - 6 months after potty training. Some may take as long as a year before they are able to stay dry throughout the night. So the best you can do is to be patient and wait for your child to develop.

What To Do When Your Child Wakes Up Wet In The Middle of The Night

Above all else be calm and don't punish or give your child the impression that he or she has done something wrong. Just clean them up, change their pajamas and provide a dry pair of training pants and put them back to bed.

Help Your Child Stay Dry

Limiting liquids before bed won't do much good. Instead make sure the last thing your child does as part of their bedtime routine, is go to the bathroom. If they are still awake before you hit the sack, it would be a good idea to take them to the bathroom one last time.

Issue 5: Room Sharing with a Sibling

Many parents decide to have their toddler share a room with a sibling. The reasons for doing so vary. Some have no other choice due to a lack of space. Others feel it provides companionship and may give young children a better sense of security when it's time for bed. Besides, those monsters under the bed aren't so tough when you've got a sidekick to help you get rid of them!

Is Room Sharing A Good Idea?

In theory there's nothing wrong with your toddler sharing with a sibling. The question is whether or not it can work for other reasons. If your toddler shares with an infant, it could be a problem if your two year old is very active or resistant to going to bed at night. If your toddler is disturbing an infant constantly then sharing a room is an issue.

There's no right or wrong answer. You can experiment and see how it goes. If you've mastered the art of getting your toddler to sleep without too much commotion it should work out fine.

Sharing With Another Toddler

If you opt to have two toddlers share a room it can be great for both. Some parents choose to have them share the same bed in the beginning. Or having separate beds close to each other works just as well.

Compatibility

As long as your children are compatible with each other then room sharing is fine. Eventually they will "outgrow" each other and will want their own room. In the beginning while they're very young, most children enjoy sharing rooms.

A Quick Note About Bedtime Routines When Sharing Rooms

You may have to create two separate routines depending on the ages of your children. An older toddler may have different needs than a younger sibling and the routines should reflect those differences. One may need to go to bed earlier or later than the other. Based on age, personality and their stage of development, create routines for each.

Issue 6: Early Risers

Once your little angel is sleeping through the night you breathe a sigh of relief until they start waking up way too early in the morning.

Here are a few strategies you can use to teach your child when it's okay to get up each morning. Obviously this is for toddlers 2 years and older.

Watch The Clock

There are all kinds of sleep training clocks you can purchase that can help you teach your child about getting up in the mornings. Among my favorites are the clocks with colorful animated pictures of a character asleep or awake. You will set the clock to change the picture from sleeping to waking at a specific time. The clock won't ring like an alarm it will just change the picture your child sees.

Make it a game with your child. Show your child the funny pictures and explain when the character is sleeping he or she should sleep too. When the character on the clock is showing as awake, then it's okay for your child to get out of bed. Then have some fun practicing until he or she begins to make the connection.

It may take several mornings before your child figures it all out so be patient. If your child is getting up at 5 a.m. now, setting the clock for 8 a.m. is not going to work. You'll have to make the time change gradual. Eventually, your child will adjust and either sleep longer or wait until the clock shows them that they can wake up and get out of bed.

Make Some Adjustments

In addition to the clock you can make sure your child's room at least gives the impression it is still night. Light blocking curtains will keep the room dark enough so your child thinks it's still nighttime and they should go back to sleep.

Experiment with bedtimes. It could be they are going to bed too early. Try extending bedtime by an hour and see if that helps.

The next time your toddler wakes up too early, try taking him or her back to their bed and calmly let them know it's too early for mommy and daddy. You can also get a night light with a timer. Teach your child to sleep in their room until the light comes on.

Another option is to return them to their room and allow them to play with their toys with the door closed until you return.

Young Toddlers Still Breastfeeding

Nighttime feeding for young toddlers still breastfeeding can be exhausting for moms. If you're ready to wean your toddler from nighttime feeding be sure your child is ready to do so.

A good rule of thumb is to first check with your child's pediatrician. The average child between 4 and 6 months old should be getting more than enough of the required nutrients needed for growth and healthy development, so ending nighttime feeding shouldn't be an issue. Let your child's pediatrician know you want to discontinue nighttime breastfeeding. If your child gets the thumbs up medically then proceed with the following strategy.

Weaning Toddlers Off Nighttime Breastfeeding

Try feeding your child several times a few hours before bedtime. Do so close together. This way your child should not wake up hungry and will sleep for longer periods of time.

It's important to understand that breastfeeding for your child is more than just a source of food for them. It is also a precious bond that gives them a lot of comfort and security. They associate breastfeeding with something that makes them feel good. You will have to find other ways to give comfort.

Sometimes just the gentle sound of your voice and a stroke of their forehead is enough to lull them back to sleep. You should make this nighttime interaction short and sweet. Even with their eyes closed they can smell you and may get too distracted to sleep.

When your child starts crying, do not run in immediately to quiet him or her down. Wait a few minutes and see if your child settles down without you. If they continue to cry try calming them using the method described above.

It may take a few nights or several nights to wean your child from nighttime breastfeeding but if you stay consistent eventually you'll enjoy more and more nights of uninterrupted sleep.

Nanny P

From Crib to Toddler Bed

You can make the transition from crib to toddler bed a fun event for your child. In fact by making it a big deal and a happy occasion it may help him or her adjust a bit quicker to sleeping in their new bed.

Get Them Excited!

Start the day letting your child know how special the day is for them. Tell your child they are getting to be a big boy or girl and that means they get to have their own bed!

Talk about how much fun they can have sleeping in their bed with their favorite toys or reading their books. You could even purchase some party hats beforehand and make it feel like a big party. If you choose to go to a local store to buy a toddler bed wear the party hats. The sales staff will love it and join the party!

If you choose to order online you can still keep the party theme going. Let your child sit with you in front of the computer as you look for toddler beds. You can even show him or her how to click on different beds to get a closer look.

Let Your Child Choose Their Bed

Narrow down a few beds and then let your child choose the one he or she likes the best. Stay upbeat. You can even let your child click the buy button if ordering online and then celebrate! Explain that their very own bed is on its way and will be there soon. If there is tracking information, you can make a countdown game out of it. Put up a wall chart with numbers to count down the days till the new bed arrives.

Shop For Linen & Stickers

Let your child pick out sheets, pillow cases and blankets. Buy some stickers they can use to decorate their new bed. Make the process happy and fun.

Once The Bed Arrives

Praise them on doing such a great job helping you choose the bed. Let your child help you do little things to help you set the bed up. Then let them put stickers on the bed where they want. Let them help make up the bed and get it ready for bedtime.

The more you can associate positive things with the new bed, the more you can help to decrease the anxiety your child will feel when it's time to sleep in their brand new bed for the first time.

Just keep in mind, even with all of the feel good stuff you've done it may take your child time to get used to it. Or if you're lucky, he or she may be just fine with it right from the start. Be patient and stick to your bedtime routine and it will eventually all come together.

Potential Medical Issues

Obstructive sleep apnea syndrome also known as OSAS can be a problem for some children. The symptoms of sleep apnea include the following:

Breathing through the mouth while asleep
Sleeping a lot more than normal during the day
Behavior problems caused from lack of adequate sleep
Enlarged tonsils and adenoids
Loud snoring

This sleep disorder causes disruption in a child's normal sleep pattern. If you think your child may have sleep apnea, talk to your pediatrician and have him or her evaluated as soon as possible. There are various treatments available depending on the diagnosis. If your child is overweight or has allergies, both could be causing sleep apnea. The solution could be as simple as treating the allergies or managing your child's weight with a proper diet.

The removal of your child's tonsils and adenoids is also a common solution to dealing with sleep apnea in children.

Nanny P

Dealing with Changes in Routine

At some point you will want to take your toddler with you on vacation. Depending on how far and the mode of transportation you could easily end up choosing not to stay with the normal bedtime routine. The choice to do so or not is really up to you.

However, I suggest sticking to your child's regular routine as closely as possible. If not, be prepared to "start over" by reintroducing the bedtime routine once you return home.

Children get confused very easily. They don't understand that they're on vacation. What they understand is you're now telling them they don't have to do what they've been taught to do anymore. Then once they get back home, they won't understand why you want them to change again.

Try as much as possible to maintain the same bedtime routine even while on vacation. You may not be able to do it exactly but get as close as possible.

Family & Friends

If visiting family and friends, it would be a good idea to let them know in advance about your child's routine. If everyone is on the same page it will eliminate confusion for your child later.

Time Zones

If you will be in a different time zone, make sure to make adjustments accordingly for your child. It's not likely that your toddler is running around with a watch on his or her wrist. It's up to you to make sure they're not going to bed too late or too early.

Plane Trips

Most young children get very restless on airplanes. Who can blame them! It's a small space with no place to run and play. Make sure you have some quiet toys to keep your child distracted. Many children tend to get lulled to sleep eventually. There's not a lot of leeway when it comes to flights.

Car Trips

The constant movement in long car trips can put young children to sleep. Watching DVD movies and playing with toys only lasts so long before Mr. Sandman puts them to sleep. Allow them to sleep. Getting them to sleep later may or may not be difficult. Long trips can be physically draining for young children.

Stay The Course

If you find it difficult to get them to sleep later that night, just know that it may take a few nights for your child to adjust to unfamiliar surroundings. However, you should still do your best to stick with the normal bedtime routine as much as possible.

A Word About Co-Sleeping Option

If you are a parent who chooses co-sleeping with your toddler there's nothing wrong with that decision. Some research suggests that children who sleep with their parents do not grow up feeling dependent on others. Some believe that they grow up very independent, are able to deal with stress better, are more confident and have higher self esteem. Still others find no difference between children who do sleep with their parents and those that don't.

Co-sleeping

Co-sleeping is not having your toddler sleep in the bed with you. Your child sleeps in the same room and the crib is close enough that you can simply reach out and touch it. However, some parents also use the term to describe having their toddler sleep with them in their bed.

Which methods you choose is up to you as neither method has proved to harm the development of a child in any way. One note of caution, very young toddlers under 12 months should not sleep in bed with parents due to the risk of SIDS (Sudden Infant Death Syndrome).

Sample Bedtime Routine for Co-Sleeping

Creating a bedtime routine for co-sleeping is not much different than routines for toddlers sleeping on their own.

Begin winding down for bed at least an hour before bedtime. That means no over excitement in terms of play time or television. It's fine to allow quiet play time. Then let your child help put away all of their toys for the night.

Offer a small snack. Tell your child it's time to get ready for bed.

Giving a warm bath followed by a nice rub down with lavender scented baby lotion will relax your toddler and calm them down.

Let your child pick out the pajamas they would like to wear.

Have short story time by reading from their favorite book.

If you're still breastfeeding, you may want to give one last feeding for the night.

Then lights out. Let your child fall asleep. If he or she fidgets around wait and see if they work it out on their own. If not feel free to offer some comfort to help them fall asleep.

Sweet Dreams!

Congratulations you made it!

You now have all the tools you need to get your angel to go to sleep, stay in bed and enjoy sleeping and having their own bed. Remember that every child is different and the time it will take him or her to "get it" varies from one child to the next. Stay patient, be consistent and don't give up!

Eventually, you'll see your toddler begin to have those wonderful "ah ha" moments you'll remember for many years to come. Sure it can be frustrating for you in the beginning but stay calm and focused and all will work out.

When you're ready to purchase a toddler bed, story books and training clocks be sure to check out the Resources in the next section. I've put together a list of some of the best products highly rated by parents just like you.

Nanny P

Resources

Good Books for Children

Big Enough for a Bed (Sesame Street)
http://www.amazon.com/dp/0375822704/

Best for boys | Age level 2 and up

Elmo learns all about sleeping in his own bed! Your toddler will fall in love with this simple but wonderful story. It's fully illustrated with brilliant colors to capture your child's attention. It's very short which is great, because most toddlers won't sit still for long stories. Little boys will be able to relate to Elmo as he learns about sleeping in his brand new "big boy" bed.

Your Own Big Bed
http://www.amazon.com/dp/0670060798/

Best for boys | Age level 2 and up

Rita M. Bergstein makes it a lot easier for your little boy to make the transition to sleeping in his own big bed. The author uses beautiful illustrations and stories about how animals go through different stages, get bigger and soon they leave their mom and dad and have their own special place to sleep too!

I Sleep in My Own Bed
http://www.amazon.com/dp/1453543414/

Best for both boy and girls | Age level 2 and up

What makes this book written by author Glenn Wright so special is the personal nature of the story line itself. Glenn based the character and experiences in the book based on his own son Bradley, but this book is written in a way that will appeal to both boys and girls. If you have a toddler who is resistant to the idea of sleeping in their own bed because they're afraid of those pesky monsters under the bed, this book will quickly become one of your child's favorite reads at bedtime.

The Sleep Fairy
http://www.amazon.com/dp/0971440522/

Best for both boys and girls | Age level 2 and up

This book received a Mom's Choice Award for excellence in children's books and for good reason. It focuses on one of the most frustrating issues for parents when it comes to toddlers and sleeping. Getting your child to stay in their bed at night. Author Janie Peterson does a brilliant job of weaving a delightful story that keeps your child's attention while at the same time makes your toddler look forward to "staying in bed" through the night.

It's Time to Sleep in Your Own Bed
http://www.amazon.com/dp/1572245867/

Best for both boys and girls | Age level 2 and up

This book written by child psychologist Lawrence Shapiro is about a little boy named Alex having a tough time with the idea of sleeping in his own bed. If your child has been sleeping with you in your bed, this book is a sweet story that will strike a chord with most toddlers.

Good Night, Sleep Tight Reward Chart - The Ultimate Sleep Chart for Children (2yrs+)
http://www.amazon.com/dp/B0077M92T4/

Best for both boys and girls | Age level 2 and up

Rewarding your child as he or she makes the transition to sleeping in their own bed can work wonders! This is one of the best reward charts available. You can reward your child with gold stickers when they participate in their bedtime routine. There are smiley faces for staying in their bed through the night and it also includes additional tips for you to get the most out of using a reward system successfully.

Special Clocks for Children:

Kid'sleep Classic
http://www.amazon.com/dp/B000VVIHPS/

Best for both boys and girls | Age level 3 and up (Due to small parts not a good idea for children under 3)

If you needed only one word to describe this sleep training clock it would be "Beautiful" without a doubt. The face of the clock is very colorful and your child will instantly recognize and fall in love with the cute bunny rabbit. The clock teaches your child when it's time for sleeping and when it's time to wake up and get out of bed. It's also a night light.

Kid'sleep My First Alarm Clock
http://www.amazon.com/dp/B004GHEDL0/

Best for both boys and girls | Age level 3 and up

Recommended for older toddlers. Can be used to teach your child how to tell time. It works pretty much the way a typical alarm clock works with an alarm and snooze functions. If your child isn't ready to learn how to tell time that's fine. This clock has both a regular analog face and an additional part of the clock has a colorful character of a sleeping child and a child awake. This way your child can look at the picture and learn when to sleep and when to wake up based on which picture is illuminated.

OK to Wake! Children's Alarm Clock and Nightlight
http://www.amazon.com/dp/B002RNKOM2/

Best for both boys and girls | Age level 2 and up

If your toddler insists on waking up every morning at 5 a.m. then this may be the answer to solve your problem. This clock uses color to teach your child when it's time to wake up and get out of bed. Yellow light at bed time means it's time to go to sleep. In the morning when the face turns green your toddler will learn it's okay to wake up mommy and daddy! It can grow with your child too. It also has an alarm, snooze button and night light.

My Tot Clock: Helping Small Children Sleep Better...So Parents Can Too!
http://www.amazon.com/dp/B001QS802K/

Best for both boys and girls | Age level 3 months and up

If you're looking for clock that does almost everything this is it! This sleep training clock tells time, changes colors to signal when to sleep and when to wake, plays bedtime stories, lullabies, white noise and has snappy fun wake up music too! Your toddler will not only learn about staying in their bed but can also enjoy being entertained when you're a bit too sleepy. Create your bedtime routine and set the clock accordingly.

Toddler Beds:

Dream On Me Classic Toddler Bed - White
http://www.amazon.com/dp/B001OW6K2A/

Best for boys and girls | Age level 2 and up

This toddler bed is made of wood and comes in your choice of 8 non toxic finishes. It should be suitable for the average toddler as it was designed for little ones to easily get in and out of their "new big bed!" Also comes with safety rails on each side to keep more adventurous toddlers from falling out of their new bed.

P'kilino Toddler Bed & Chair
http://www.amazon.com/dp/B001RIY7B2

Best for both boys and girls | Age level 24 months to 6 years

Not only is this a well constructed sturdy bed for your toddler it's also beautifully designed and stylish. This isn't a two piece set. The bed itself folds up into a chair! Wood construction, side rails to keep your child from falling out and fits any standard size crib mattress.

Disney Princess Toddler Bed
http://www.amazon.com/dp/B003IT79I6

Girls | 18 months to 5 years

This is the perfect little bed for your little Princess! Gorgeous pink bed with a beautiful canopy will make your child eager to spend time sleeping in her own bed. Standard crib mattress, safety side rails and low to ground to make it easy for her to get in and out of bed. Adorable!

Sesame Street Plastic Toddler Bed
http://www.amazon.com/dp/B0057GU07K

Boys | 18 months to 5 years

Your little boy will feel like a "big boy" in this very sturdy, colorful plastic and metal toddler bed featuring characters every toddler knows and loves from Sesame Street. The brightly colored plastic frame is non toxic, sturdy and uses a standard crib mattress.

Regalo My Cot Portable Bed, Royal Blue
http://www.amazon.com/dp/B000H1MRJO

Best for boys and girls | As young as 12 months and up

If you're going to be traveling, staying at relatives or in a hotel this portable toddler bed is the perfect way to make sure your child stays on their normal sleeping routine. Plus it's also great for nap time. If you have a very young toddler that will be going to a day care facility, this is a great bed to get him or her used to sleeping on day care cots. It's also a great way to transition very young toddlers from their crib to napping on a cot when they're not quite old enough to move to a full size toddler bed.

It's lightweight and folds down to almost half its size, making it very easy to travel with if necessary.

Nanny Notes on Toddlers

Nanny P's Blueprint For Raising Confident Children

Nanny P

Nanny P's Blueprint for Raising Confident Children

Nanny P

Self-Esteem vs Self-Confidence

I'm glad you've taken the time to read a book like this on building self-esteem in your young child. Unfortunately, the topic of self-esteem and self-confidence doesn't usually come up until much later after a child is already showing signs of self-esteem issues. Then it's a mad rush to get them into counseling or some kind of therapy to "fix" them.

Sure, raising children is a job and an adventure! But raising a child with positive self-esteem is a journey that should begin right from the start. When young minds are forming, they are taking in an enormous amount of information. They really are like little sponges soaking it all up. What goes on in your child's environment, from what he or she sees, hears, touches and experiences all play major roles in how your child's confidence grows. The most important thing that can build up or break down your child's self-esteem and self-confidence is you the parent, other family members including siblings, extended family and close friends.

Your child will learn to see his or herself positively or negatively based on what you say, how you act towards them and how you allow others to interact with him or her. Even if your child hasn't developed the ability to communicate fully, they are listening and learning all the time.

A friend of mine has a 2 year old and every time I would visit I would let her play a memory game on my PC. Each time I clicked on the game a window would pop up asking if I wanted to open up a previously saved game. It gives a choice of yes or no and I always clicked no. I would then allow the 2 year old to play. The next time I visited she insisted on starting the game. To my surprise she went to the correct icon and clicked. When the information window popped up she clicked no and proceeded to play the game.

She could not read but she had watched me click the no button enough times that she had learned how to get past that window.

The point I'm trying to make is, never assume your child is not paying attention to what's being said or can't figure it out.

You might be surprised.

Self-Esteem From A - Z

What Is Self-Esteem?

The definition of self-esteem is the same for a child as it is for an adult. Basically it is how one views him or herself. It is what they believe to be true even if it isn't. Generally, a child with a healthy self view of themselves will develop into a well adjusted confident adult.

Your child's self-esteem will form and change during various stages of their development. Most parents focus on the things they can see when it comes to growing children. That is physical changes, verbal skills, eating habits etc. Monitoring a child's self-esteem growth isn't always of great concern until there is a noticeable problem. I think it's because most parents don't really think about nurturing self-esteem. It's not because they don't care, it's just something they don't think about until their child is older. Typically many parents focus on self-esteem issues when kids are old enough to attend school and self-confidence issues become a lot more apparent.

If you take preventative steps now while your child is young, you may be able to avoid more serious issues with self-esteem when they are older. The overall goal is to help your child feel better about him or herself and to feel more confident.

Low Self-esteem Can Cause Problems

When a child has a healthy view of themselves they will react to their world a lot more confidently. But if their self-esteem is low their behavior can be difficult or they may have a hard time communicating and socializing with other children as well as with adults.

If left unchecked, a child with low self-esteem can carry those same issues into adulthood.

For example, if your child grows up believing he or she isn't smart enough and steps aren't taken to help them form a new view of themselves, they will go through life thinking they can't excel not only in education but in a career as well. For example, your child may avoid looking for a better paying job because their false self-esteem has them believing they don't have what it takes.

Low self-esteem can lead to a lifetime of relationship problems with future spouses, family members, friends and coworkers.

How Does Your Child Form Their Self-esteem?

Remember when I mentioned in the first section about how young children are like "sponges" soaking up everything in their environment? Not only are they learning how to communicate, they are also reacting to their environment. How they react to something can be a strong indication of whether or not they have high or low self-esteem.

For instance, notice how your child reacts to loud noises. If he or she is curious and goes toward the sound to learn more about it, that's a good sign that they are feeling confident and aren't too bothered by the sound. If, on the other hand, you notice your child seems to be afraid and runs away, it's an indication your child may be forming a negative association with loud noises.

Every child is different but in this example it's possible a child could form an unnatural fear of loud noises that could also make him or her uncomfortable when trying out new things in their life. It doesn't have to be just about the noise. It can extend to being afraid to try or experience new things in general.

Why It's Important To Help Your Child With Self-esteem Issues As Early As Possible

If you noticed your child limping, you would immediately take the proper steps to find out what was wrong. You would check for wounds or possible broken bones. A trip to the doctor might also be the next thing you do. The point is, you would do whatever is necessary to help your child to feel better.

You should feel the same way when it comes to their self-esteem. The more confident your child is about who they are and how they see themselves, the better they will be able to handle the challenges they will face throughout their life.

Spotting self-esteem issues in your child can be pretty easy if you know what to look for.

Signs Your Child May Be Suffering From Low Self-esteem

The best way to figure out if your child has self-esteem issues is to listen closely to your child when he or she is communicating with you or others.

Ages 2-4 years

"I don't like me."
"I can't do that like her."
"I can't learn that!"

Other signs can include:

Refusing to follow your rules and push the limits as much as they can.

Very young toddlers will be verbally challenged and you may have to rely more on their body language.

Your child may shy away from playing with other children.

If you notice your child has a problem sharing toys for example they may have a confidence problem that stems from poor self-esteem.

Healthy Self-Esteem

Very social and interacts well with others.
Enjoys learning new things.
Happy to follow the rules.

There are different factors that contribute to how a child will ultimately view themselves.

Environment

How your child interacts both at home and away can be one of the factors that shapes your child's self-esteem. What your child is exposed to in terms of attitudes and how they're treated play a major role in how they eventually see themselves.

Social Interactions

Interactions with other children and adults. How your child plays with other children and socializes also helps him or her form an opinion about themselves. It's in these kinds of interactions where your child will compare him or herself to others. They will also develop their communication skills. If your child is uncomfortable meeting new people, it may be a sign they need help feeling confident in social situations. On the other hand, a child that has no problem going right up to children they don't know tends to be a lot more confident.

Self-Esteem In Babies And Toddlers

9 months

Believe it or not children begin to form opinions about themselves even when they're babies. Children under 2 years of age look for confirmation about themselves in the way you respond to them.

For example, when a baby smiles or coos they love it when you respond cooing and smiling too. It lets them know it's okay to feel that way and they will continue that behavior because they like it.

Playing games and interacting with you to get your attention is another way they form a sense of self. If you ignore them when they reach for you or attempt to play games like peek-a-boo, they will begin to feel rejection. Not getting attention at this early critical age, can lead to them believing they're not good enough.

18 months – 2 years

Around 18 months of age, a child begins to explore their environment more and challenge your authority. It's during this time that it is most crucial to be careful as to how you react to your child's behavior. If your child misbehaves, gently but firmly remind your child of what the rules are and then redirect his or her behavior.

For example, if your child knows that it's inappropriate to play with the television remote but decides to disobey the rule, remind him or her gently and then redirect their attention to something that is allowed. But whatever you do, no yelling or criticizing. During the 18 months to 2 year window, toddlers are extremely sensitive. Negative reactions and anger towards them can be devastating to their self-esteem.

Next, let's take a look at your role as a parent in building your child's self-esteem.

Nanny P

Your Role As A Parent

As a parent, it's important to recognize your role in the healthy self-esteem of your child. Your child looks to you for everything in their life. You are the center of their universe. They learn from watching and listening to you. So it's really important to treat the task of raising a child with healthy self-esteem with the same level of importance you would for anything else regarding your child.

Be careful how you speak around your child. Be mindful of the tone and words you use when speaking to your child. An easy way to find out what your child is absorbing from you and others in the household is to listen to how they speak to other children or even to themselves when playing alone.

If you notice your child is being mean to another child and yelling, it is most likely because that is what they are used to hearing in your household. If they hear arguing all the time they will mimic having an argument. All young children talk to inanimate objects especially when they're playing alone. They will act out and speak to a doll or favorite teddy bear in much the same way they are spoken to as well.

As the parent you need to be the positive example for your child.

Create A Goal

Working with your child's self-esteem is something that will be ongoing until they leave "the nest" and so your goals will change as your child matures.

However, in the beginning while they are very young you can create a positive healthy foundation and adjust as you need to. The adjustments will vary from one child to the next depending on their environment and the kinds of messages they are exposed to on a daily basis.

Don't worry about being perfect or making mistakes. You're not going to do everything right but by focusing on helping your child to be more confident, you will be more aware of what is working and what isn't.

Now before we get into some positive self-esteem building strategies you can use, here are a few examples of things you should not do.

Don't Make Demands Too Big For Your Child To Handle

Be careful not to put too much pressure on your child to succeed at something. Instead, be aware of what their limitations are and allow him or her to do the best they can on their own level. Constantly telling a child that they're not trying hard enough can cause him or her to doubt their ability to do things in life as they get older.

No Criticizing Or Yelling

Have you ever witnessed a parent yelling at a toddler in a restaurant or other public area? Screaming at a child because they're not behaving in a certain way is bad and any parent should refrain from doing so. Yelling at a child in front of others can cause a child to feel embarrassed and can have a negative effect on how they interact with people as they get older. Adults who routinely belittle others most likely do so because they were belittled as a child. Of course your child could encounter this behavior from others, but if you're consistently focusing on raising your child within a healthy confident environment. They will be able to handle negative situations from others better as they mature.

Name Calling And Harsh Words

Most parents wouldn't dream of calling their small child or any child for that matter something that would hurt and demean them. Unfortunately, it happens all the time. We've all been around a child that seems determined to drive us crazy by doing something that just gets on our nerves. The key is not to react negatively and resort to calling them dumb, stupid or lazy for example.

A good friend of mine told me he was out running some errands one afternoon and decided to grab a bite to eat. While standing in line, another customer purchased some food and proceeded to give his young son who looked to be about 3 or 4, a cup of soda to hold as they walked to a table to sit down.

The child accidentally dropped the soda and the Dad went ballistic. He started yelling at the child, telling him he was clumsy and that he'll never let him carry sodas anymore! My friend who is the father of 3 boys decided to intervene.

He calmly walked over and in a calm but stern voice told the Dad to calm down. My friend went on to tell him that it was his fault for expecting a little child to have enough control to hold on to a drink in the first place. At that point my friend said the guy told him to mind his own business, gathered up his kid and left.

I wish that story had a better ending but the unfortunate truth is that kind of behavior happens and that child will most likely grow up with low self-esteem.

If you have a tendency to "lose it" when something doesn't go the way you want, you'll have to learn to not take it out on your child.

Words that hurt can be devastating to a child. Especially if those words come from the one person your child loves unconditionally.

You.

So I can't stress enough how important it is to never describe your child as being dumb or saying things like you wish they were never born. You probably would never say such things but believe it or not there are parents who do and many don't realize the harm that they are doing.

Even your attitude towards them can make a big difference. Giving a child the silent treatment hurts. If you get angry with your child, you need to do whatever is necessary to calm down and gather yourself. Then have a calm talk with your child and discuss ways he or she can improve their behavior. Let him or her know you're there to support them and how much you appreciate it when they follow the rules and act accordingly.

Nanny P

Strategies For Boosting Self-Esteem In Your Child

Raising happy children with a positive outlook about themselves and the world they live in can be tough. That's because children are exposed to so much from so many different sources it can be quite overwhelming. That's why it's so important to start your child off with a good solid foundation when they're very young and continue until they one day leave to live life on their own.

In the next sections you'll learn some simple strategies that will help your child to grow into a confident adult. Some strategies you may be using already and others you may not have given much thought about. So make sure you read each one and use only the ones that make sense for you and your child.

Strategy 1: Encouragement & Praise
Strategy 2: Show Genuine Interests In Your Child's Activities
Strategy 3: Focus On The Positive
Strategy 4: Listen To What Your Child Has To Say
Strategy 5: Encourage Dreams
Strategy 6: Encourage Independence
Strategy 7: Don't Forget To Say "I Love You!"
Strategy 8: Stop Telling Your Child What They Should Not Do
Strategy 9: Consistent Boundaries & Discipline
Strategy 10: Let Your Child Know That Everyone Fails Sometimes
Strategy 11: Monitor What Your Child Is Exposed To
Strategy 12: Show Off Your Child's Artistic Flare!
Strategy 13: Play Dates & Socialization Skills

Nanny P

Strategy 1: Encouragement & Praise

Encouraging your child whenever he or she is trying something new or learning how to do something they've never done before is crucial to building positive self-esteem. Even if it's something small like stacking their toys neatly each evening before bed.

Your child may not get it right the first time, the 10th time or the 50th time and that's okay. Children want to please their parents and they love it when you tell them they've done a good job. So instead of pointing out what they did wrong praise them for what they did right. Congratulate your child and let them know how proud you are of what they have accomplished.

When you see your child getting frustrated because they're having difficulties getting something done, praise your child for trying, then help him or her with whatever they're trying to do. Give lots of positive praise and let your child know how proud of them you are for trying and not giving up. Engage your child by asking what he or she needs help with and ask if it would be okay if you help. Don't get upset if he or she says they don't want your help. It's just a sign that your child is very independent and wants to figure it out on their own. Just be ready if your child changes their mind and wants help later. It will be important to be positive and offer help. By doing so you are teaching your child that it's okay to ask for help when they need it and that there's nothing to be ashamed about.

When positive reinforcement and praise become a consistent part of their experience it will give your child more confidence to try new things.

Nanny P

Strategy 2: Show Genuine Interests In Your Child's Activities

Even young children have things they like to do and want to share those experiences with you. What may seem like an uneventful activity to you may mean the world to your child. So ask them questions about whatever they're doing.

Stacking toy blocks might be a major architectural event to your child. Having a tea party may be the social event of the year!

As your child gets older they will be a lot more comfortable inviting you to help them with things like school projects. When your child becomes a young adult and has to deal with the normal challenges in life, they are more likely to come to you for advice. That's because they will have fond memories of the times you spent getting involved with things that mattered most to them at the time.

Just be careful not to insist on giving them help. Allow your child to make that decision.

Sometimes just knowing you care about what is important to them is enough to boost their self-esteem.

Nanny P

Strategy 3: Focus On The Positive

From the time children are very young, even before they're able to communicate verbally, they have the ability to tell the difference between positive and negative actions.

So it's important to find something positive to say about your child as much as possible. For example, whenever I see a young child wearing glasses, I make it a point to mention how fantastic they look wearing their glasses. It always brings a warm smile and a thank you. The reason I do this is because it can be tough for a young child wearing glasses because other children tend to tease them. It can make them feel self-conscious about themselves.

Always find positive comments to make about something your child likes to do, the clothes they're wearing and even the choices they make.

Another example…when you notice your child doing something helpful be sure to let them know how much you appreciate what they've done.

One of my nephews loves to share whatever he has with other children. If he has candy, he will go out of his way to make sure everyone else has candy too. Each time I see him sharing, I tell him how great it is to share and look after his friends.

Here's another example.

If your child loves a certain sport but isn't as good as other children, compliment him or her on the skills they do have. There's a great television commercial that features a young boy about 8 years of age. He is doing his best to hit a baseball over and over again. He shouts "I'm the greatest hitter in the world!" He keeps trying enthusiastically until finally he realizes he is not very good at hitting the baseball and switches to pitching instead. He then begins shouting "I'm the greatest pitcher in the world!"

It's one of the best examples of a child with healthy self-esteem. The sports example can also be applied to just about anything else. If your child isn't the best when it comes to math, let him or her know you're there to help them and just to do the best they can. Then be sure to compliment and praise them on how good they are in other subjects.

Strategy 4: Listen To What Your Child Has To Say

Even a very young child needs you to listen to them. Take the time to sit down and encourage your child to talk about whatever may be on their mind. With older children this is extremely important because they are going through a lot of changes socially and physically. They may be feeling awkward about their looks, their body and even their intelligence. Be supportive and point out their good qualities.

When it comes to toddlers, their communication skills are obviously limited but that doesn't mean they don't have anything to say. Toddlers can communicate about how they are feeling and even how they are feeling about someone else by their actions.

For example, a good friend of mine has a set of twin boys. When they were about 2 years old she noticed one of her sons was outgoing and loved to play outside, but his twin seemed to be extremely afraid of something outside. Whenever she would open the door he would run and hide. So she asked him what was wrong and why he was afraid, but he couldn't verbalize what was bothering him. After observing his behavior more closely she began to see a pattern. Her son only seemed afraid when it was a bright sunny day. His fear as it turned out was fear of the sun!

She took steps to ease his fears and made sure he wasn't teased by his brother. Eventually his fear of the sun went away and he was the first one out the door ready for a day of play!

Now although his fear of the sun was irrational, it was for whatever reason scary for him. By helping her son work through his fear by not making fun of him and allowing him to get through it at his own pace, he was able to "grow out" of it.

Your child may have fears about something and they need you to listen and comfort them. Or they may be having a difficult time trying to understand how something works. Maybe another child or adult is making them feel bad about themselves. Whatever it is, listen and do whatever it takes to understand and help them deal with the situation accordingly.

The adage that "children should be seen and not heard" is no longer good advice.

So never take what your child is trying to communicate to you for granted. To your child, it's the most important thing in the world and to him or her, you are probably the only one who can make them feel better.

Strategy 5: Encourage Dreams

Some of the world's most inspiring ideas and inventions became a reality because those individuals had self-confidence and a positive view of themselves and their abilities.

If your child has a big dream to become something or create some new invention, no matter how far-fetched it may sound to you it's important to be encouraging and not make him or her feel as if their dreams are too big or too difficult to achieve.

When I was a young kid my parents always encouraged me to dream big and always supported me in whatever I chose to do. Even if your child wants to be the first woman to win a NASCAR race one week and a doctor the next week, support them and help them make decisions. Show interest in their dreams and really invest time and effort in helping them.

Schedule time to help them accomplish their goals and work toward their dreams. In the case of very young children if they tell you they want to grow up to be a teacher, a fireman or some other profession, you can purchase toys and games that help to support their interests.

Allow them to use play time to be what they dream of. There are thousands of adults who will tell you they dreamed of being a police officer, nurse, truck driver or even an entrepreneur since they were as young as 4 or 5.

It's never too early to support your child's dreams.

Nanny P

Strategy 6: Encourage Independence

When a child has confidence to try new things and accomplish tasks put before them, it sets the stage for building a stronger healthy self-esteem. You can begin this process when your child is very young. From the time your child begins to walk you can encourage independence by letting him or her take steps on their own. When he or she falls down, don't make a big deal about it. Instead praise your child for trying and tell them how proud you are of them.

Reward them with affection.

When your child is hesitant to try something let him or her know that it's okay to check it out. Encourage your child to play with new toys and play with other children. Increasing your child's social skills will also help him or her to be more independent.

Try taking your child to new places to experience new sounds and sights. For young children, your local Children's Museum is a great place to see, feel, hear and touch new things. Getting involved in outside activities will help build confidence and allow them to learn more about themselves and the world around them.

Allow your child to explore their environment while you supervise to make sure they do so safely. Talk to them about what they're experiencing and ask questions. Your genuine interest will further help them to feel more confident in their choices as they go along.

Other activities that encourage independence include helping you do things around the house. Let your child help set the table for dinner, take the trash out or put their toys away each night. Then make sure you tell them how much you appreciate their help. In time they will want to do those tasks completely on their own. That will be a sure sign that they are becoming more self-confident and comfortable with doing things independently.

Nanny P

Strategy 7: Don't Forget To Say "I Love You"

You can never tell your child that you love them too many times. A loving environment is important even when your child disobeys you or does something else that goes against your rules. While you must maintain consistency when it comes to discipline, it is even more important to let your child know they are loved even when they do something you disapprove of.

As your child gets older and they begin to experience challenges in their lives, he or she will feel better and will be able to deal with life's ups and downs knowing you love them no matter what.

At some point as your child gets older, they may seem to not be interested so much in getting a lot of affection. This can be especially true with young boys. Don't worry about it and don't stop. They may pretend they don't want your affection but they do.

Nanny P

Strategy 8: Stop Telling Your Child What They Should Not Do

One of the most common mistakes parents make is constantly telling their child what they should not do.

Here's why that is a problem.

When you're always telling a child what they should not do then they have a difficult time figuring what they should do on their own. As they get older they will find it harder to make confident decisions on their own and will instead look for someone else to tell them what to do.

Have you ever met someone who can't seem to make a decision about anything? Or maybe you've encountered co-workers who can't be trusted to make a decision about a work project because they need someone else to tell them what should be done?

If you instead make it a practice to tell your child what to do in various situations they will in time learn to look for solutions to problems and such on their own.

Say: "Walk into the room" instead of saying " Don't run into the room!"

Say: "Ride your bike with both hands on the handlebars" instead of saying "Don't ride your bike with one hand."

Can you see the difference?

Constantly saying "don't do this or that" doesn't help your child learn to think in a way that is positive. Think about it. If you were working on a project at your place of employment and your supervisor was constantly calling you saying, "Don't write the report like that, don't email the file like this, don't do this and that." Wouldn't that drive you nuts?

Wouldn't you feel like your boss didn't appreciate you or thought much of your ability to get the job done?

Keep this in mind when you're speaking to your child.

Strategy 9: Consistent Boundaries & Discipline

Ever been out in public and witnessed a child throwing a temper tantrum? Have you ever watched the reaction from most parents? Usually they are standing there yelling at their child to stop acting out and to stop what they're doing. Another common reaction is to stand their and try to "bargain" with the child to stop. Some parents resort to promising to buy them something they want or to take them to their favorite restaurant if they stop the tantrum.

If your child likes throwing tantrums when they don't get what they want, avoid using the tactics mentioned above. Children learn how to push your buttons and will do so to get what they want. Sometimes I think they all belong to some secret club that shares all the secrets on how to get whatever they want from their parents!

You Have To Set Limits

In the above scenarios the parent is allowing the child to set the boundaries or limits. As a parent you have to set limits on what you will and will not allow in terms of behavior from your child. Every child wants to be disciplined but they don't have the mental capacity to tell you that. Without rules of acceptable conduct, it creates a lot of stressful energy. That energy build up has to be released. Throwing tantrums, telling you no, and other defiant behavior is often the result.

When you set the rules and consistently remind your child to follow them accordingly or face the consequences, you are teaching your child about being responsible for the actions they take. Gradually they will feel more confident in their ability to make better choices and think about the consequences if they choose to break your rules.

Consequences & Discipline

We live in a society filled with boundaries, laws and limits to what we can and cannot do. If we choose to ignore those boundaries then we risk suffering the consequences. So by instilling this concept in your child early on, you are teaching them a valuable life lesson that he or she will have to deal with throughout their adult life. Unfortunately, the penal system is filled with individuals who grew up without boundaries and discipline and the consequences are harsh.

To teach your child about consequences and discipline you must be consistent. That means every time your child chooses to push the limits and ignore your boundaries you have to discipline them with a specific set of consequences every time. It's the only way your child is going to learn the importance of such.

One strategy is to simply give them a "time out" and have your child sit in a special chair you designate for specific amount of time. You could also send them to their room for 5 - 10 minutes. The consequence of spending 5 - 10 minutes in time out may not seem like much to you as an adult, but to a child that 5 - 10 minutes will feel like eternity!

Discipline No No's

Yelling, name calling and hitting a child should never be used as a form of discipline. According to research by the American Psychological Association, hitting or spanking a child can not only lead to physical injuries but also increased aggression and antisocial behavior.

Emotional scars can stay with a child for the rest of his or her life. Never discipline your child when you're angry. It's during anger that some of the most hurtful words and physical punishment take place.

Remember Love

Strategy 7 reminds you to always tell your children how much you love them. Even when you have to discipline them it's important they they understand why they are being placed in time out. It's just as important to let them know it doesn't change your love for them.

Strategy 10: Let Your Child Know That Everyone Fails Sometimes

As a parent you love seeing your child succeed at something. It could be taking their first steps, speaking their first words and a long list of other first time events. It's also common for a parent to do everything they can to keep their child from experiencing failure.

Perhaps it's because as adults we know what it feels like to fail and we don't like it. So it makes sense that as a parent you want to spare your little angel from feeling the negative emotions associated with failure.

Unfortunately, this is a big mistake that many parents make especially with toddlers.

To understand why it's a mistake let's look at game playing for example.

Have you ever played a game with your child and purposely let him or her win?

Most parents do this all the time because they don't have the heart to see their child disappointed. It's a sincere gesture that on the surface seems like the right thing to do. However, if you let your child win he or she will eventually believe they are only supposed to win and never lose. When your child plays a game for example with another child and loses, he or she may react negatively and become a sore loser. This can lead to self-esteem issues where your child begins to see himself as not being good enough to win.

To avoid this, don't let your child win just to make him or her feel good. When your child loses, focus on what they did well during the game and tell them how proud you are that they can play so well. It would also be a good idea to explain to your toddler that it's okay if they lose the game. Encourage them to keep practicing and they will get better and better.

By emphasizing their strengths and not focusing on the failure, your child will learn they won't win every single time they play, but when they lose it's not a bad thing and they shouldn't get down on themselves about it or get angry. Do so in an enthusiastic happy tone of voice. This is done to get your child to associate positive feelings with game play even when they lose.

Over time your child will begin to understand that sometimes they win and sometimes they lose and to not let it affect them to the point where they begin to have a lower opinion of themselves.

In the beginning your child may get angry or even cry when they lose. That's a clear sign that your child hasn't learned about winning and losing and it will be extremely important to work on changing their perception about losing.

Monitor Your Child When Playing With Other Children

Pay attention when your toddler is playing games with other children. Notice whether or not he or she is able to play without getting upset if they lose. If you see your child going into "sore loser mode" interrupt their play immediately and explain to them why their behavior is unacceptable.

Here's an example:

If your child begins to protest because they lost the game you might say this:

"It's so nice of you to have your friend over to play with you and I'm glad you're having so much fun. How about playing again so you can have more fun?"

Again you are associating something positive to the outcome win or lose, he or she can still have fun.

Consistency is the key here if you want to see positive results. Eventually your child will learn that losing is just something that happens and it's okay. It may be tough for you to see your little one struggling but it's better for him or her to learn this valuable life lesson now. Otherwise it will carry over into adulthood and can cause significant problems in their life.

Nanny P

Strategy 11: Monitor What Your Child Is Exposed To

There are a lot of things fighting to get your child's attention. Many of which can end up affecting how your child views themselves. Images on television capture the attention of children easily and can be very powerful.

Television

It's a good idea to limit the amount of television your child watches. Young children cannot differentiate between what's real and what's fake. Make an effort to only allow them to watch positive programming.

For very young children programs like Sesame Street, Dora The Explorer, The Doodle Bops and other shows like these, do an excellent job of teaching positive self-esteem as well as social and verbal skills.

Internet

Children as young as 3 years old are learning to use computers. Look for PC games that educate and also help your child learn about being proud of who they are.

Spend time regularly watching the programs with your child and explain anything they may have questions about.

Video Games

This should go without saying, avoid games that depict violence.

Nanny P

Strategy 12: Show Off Your Child's Artistic Flair!

You can help your child build their self-esteem by putting things they've created on display where everyone can see them. It doesn't matter if it's a finger painting or something made out of Popsicle sticks. To your child it is a masterpiece and it is something they are most likely very proud of.

Make Time To Create With Your Child

Set aside time to spend with your child and help him or her to create something. You can purchase crayons and paper. Toddlers need a lot of space when using things like crayons to draw. That's because their muscles have not developed enough to allow them to draw as accurately as an adult. Opt for the larger size drawing pads to give your little Picasso plenty room to create.

If drawing isn't something your child likes to do, look for age appropriate toys that allow them to build things. LEGOS come in all shapes and sizes and there are several created specifically for toddlers. They can put the pieces together however they see fit. Also Fisher Price makes some of the best age appropriate toys for toddlers. You can find lots of ideas through them as well.

Another idea is to purchase a white board along with special markers made specifically for them. There are all kinds of styles and sizes. You can get small portable boards or much larger ones that can hang on a wall. The ink wipes away easily and can be used over and over again.

It can be a fun option for toddlers because they can change their drawings everyday if they want. Most toddles also get a kick out of wiping the board clean and watching everything "magically" disappear.

These are just a few ideas to get you started.

Once your child has created something let him or her know how proud you are of them and how much you love what they've created. If it's a drawing or painting, hang it up and tell your child how great it looks. Compliment them on the colors and tell them how happy it makes you feel.

You may want to designate a specific area in your home where you routinely display your child's creations.

This can provide a major boost to their self-esteem. Your enthusiastic praise will make them feel confident, excited and proud of what they have accomplished. It may also give them a sense of independence because they made it all by themselves.

Strategy 13: Play Dates & Socialization Skills

Taking steps to make sure your child has a healthy self-esteem can prevent future problems. Having the ability to interact with other children and adults without feeling afraid or overly shy comes down to your child's level of confidence in themselves.

When it comes to playing with children, I think early socialization is crucial to your child's ability to communicate and learn how to conduct themselves in various social situations. A great way to accomplish this is to schedule play dates. It can be as easy as getting together with other parents with toddlers and arranging to meet on specific day and time every week.

Location

Choose a location that is child friendly like a park or you could take turns meeting at each other's homes. Having a different location is a good way to allow your child to experience different environments. It will help him or her to feel confident about encountering new places.

Other ideas to consider include:

Going to the zoo, aquarium or a local children's muscum.

Kid friendly restaurants. Usually there is a miniature playground on the premises, bright colors and lots of things to get your child's attention and stimulate curiosity.

Place of Worship - If you share a common religion with the other parents, many places of worship also have facilities for parents to bring their children for play time.

Plan

You and the other parents could plan specific activities or just choose to meet and allow the children to just play on their own.

Observe

Watch how your child interacts with the other children. Some children are eager to jump right in and start playing while others need time to warm up to playing. So make a mental note of your child's demeanor. Is he or she joining in on the fun or are they on the sideline watching. Don't confuse a child's choice to play alone as being just independent.

If your child can play happily by themselves when they're at home that's one thing and it does show they are independent and can play alone if there are no other options. If, on the other hand, your child seems pensive and uncomfortable or is clinging to you for dear life, you need to take steps to work with your child to build their self-esteem.

How?

Talk to your child and ask why they don't want to play with the other children. You can encourage your child to play and interact with the other kids but don't force them to play if they don't want to do so. Your child may need time to adjust. Having consistent play dates will eventually allow your child to feel more comfortable because they will know what to expect and will eventually get used to socializing. If your child is shy about interacting with other kids, it's your responsibility to help him or her conquer whatever fear is keeping them from enjoying play time.

It may take some time to figure out why your child is having issues or he or she may simply do a complete turnaround on their own. Every child has their own way of working things out. The most important thing you can do for your child while they are going through changes is to let them know you love them no matter what and that you're there if they need you.

Another thing to keep an eye on is your child's socialization skills. Watch how they play with other children. Do they play fairly or are they bullying other children? Observe how they communicate. Are they polite or rude?

If you see or hear your child doing or saying something inappropriate, correct the behavior right then and there. Young minds have very short attention spans and even shorter short term memories. If you wait a couple of hours later to correct something they did, your child will have no idea or concept about what you're talking about. So remind your child of the appropriate behavior while it's happening. Behaviors, both good and bad, become habit. Keep that in mind if you're trying to teach your child to stop doing something that is inappropriate. It is going to take time for new habits to form. So be consistent and be sure to reward them with praise every time they choose the appropriate behavior.

It's amazing what you will learn about your child when they are in a totally different environment and their minds are focused on other things. Don't be surprised if your child does something on a play date that you've never seen them say or do before. Just remember they are learning and soaking it all up. Just be there to show them the right path to take and it will all pay off in time.

Nanny P

Start Today And Create A Brighter Future For Your Child!

The sooner you begin the process of self-esteem building with your child, the better. The choices you make now can have a major impact on how your child lives their life as an adult.

The choices he or she makes as they get older will stem from the lessons they learned from you and their environment. That doesn't mean your child won't have challenges and it doesn't mean they won't experience failures.

What's important to keep in mind is that they will have a solid foundation that will allow them to work through problems they will encounter in life with a healthy self-esteem. They will look at themselves as someone who is intelligent and confident. They will not be overly concerned with comparing their physical attributes to that of someone else because they will be comfortable in their own skin.

They will remember the lessons, the conversations and the care you took to show the way to a positive view of who they are. They will go on to have healthy relationships and raise their children the way they were raised and lead normal happy lives.

Isn't that what we all want for our children?

You have strategies you can put to use in your child's life every day. Use them wisely and the results will speak for themselves

Nanny P

Next Steps

I hope that you've enjoyed "Nanny Notes on Toddlers".

I'd really love to hear from you!

I very much appreciate your reviews and comments so thank you in advance for taking a moment to leave one for this book:

We're in this together and I want you to know that you have a cheerleader in Nanny P!

Good luck on raising a confident and happy toddler! I know that this can be a rewarding experience for both of you.

Please visit the sites below for more tips, information and resources.

Download my FREE gift to you - "Fun Activities For Young Kids!" (And to be notified of new titles and special offers)

NannyP.com

Nanny P's Tips for Parents on FaceBook
http://www.facebook.com/meetnannyp

Twitter
http://twitter.com/MeetNannyP

Sincerely,
Nanny P

Books For Kids

I also publish books for kids under the pen name PJ Ryan. Many of these books are now available as E-books, audio and paperback (the bundles). Visit this site for audio samples and all the details:

PJRyanBooks.com
****

"Rebekah - Girl Detective"
#1 The Mysterious Garden
#2 Alien Invasion
#3 Magellan Goes Missing
#4 Ghost Hunting
#5 Grown-Ups Out To Get Us?!
#6: The Missing Gems
#7: Swimming With Sharks?!
#8: Magic Gone Wrong!
#9: Mystery At Summer Camp
#10: Zombie Burgers
#11: Mouse's Secret
#12: The Missing Ice Cream
#13: The Ghost Snowman
#14: Monkey Business
#15: Science Magic
#16: Quiet On The Set!

"Mouse's Secret Club"
#1: Let It Snow (Inside the Gym!)
#2: Haunted Playground
#3: Spotted!
#4: Magnificent Marvin
#5: Picnic Prank
#6: Fun House
#7: It's A Bird!
#8: Mouse Ninja!

"RJ - Boy Detective"
#1: The Mysterious Crate
#2: Vampire Hunting
#3: Alien Goo!
#4: Mystery Poo
#5: Mr. Pip Is Missing!
#6: Where Is Hensely?
#7: Night Noises
#8: The Cheese Thief

"Rebekah, Mouse & RJ: Special Editions"
Prank Gone Wrong
Halloween Haunted House
Thanksgiving Turkey Trouble
Christmas Party Mystery
Birthday Surprise
Happy New Year!
Playing Cupid: A Valentine's Day Surprise
Leprechaun Hunting: A St. Patrick's Day Mystery
The Easter Egg Hunt

Legal Notices and Disclaimers:

ALL RIGHTS RESERVED
No part of this book may be altered in any form whatsoever, electronic or otherwise, including photocopying, recording, or by any informational storage or retrieval system without express written, dated and signed permission from the author.

DISCLAIMER AND/OR LEGAL NOTICES
The information presented here represents the view of the author as of the date of publication. Because of the rate with which conditions change, the author reserves the right to alter and update her opinion based on new conditions as applicable. This book is for informational purposes only. While every attempt has been made to verify the information provided in this book, neither the author nor her affiliates/partners assume any responsibility for errors, inaccuracies or omissions. Any slights of people or organizations are unintentional. You should be aware of any laws which govern business transactions or other business practices in your country and state. Any reference to any person or business whether living or dead is purely coincidental.

The purchaser or reader of this publication assumes responsibility for the use of these materials and information. Adherence to all applicable laws and regulations, federal, state, and local, governing professional licensing, business practices, advertising, and all other aspects of doing business in the United States or any other jurisdiction is the sole responsibility of the purchaser or reader.

The author and publisher assume no responsibility or liability whatsoever on the behalf of any purchaser or reader of these materials.

www.ingramcontent.com/pod-product-compliance
Lightning Source LLC
Chambersburg PA
CBHW071709090426
42738CB00009B/1717